Charles Barnard

Zegelda Romanief

A Story About Music

Charles Barnard

Zegelda Romanief
A Story About Music

ISBN/EAN: 9783744693981

Printed in Europe, USA, Canada, Australia, Japan

Cover: Foto ©Thomas Meinert / pixelio.de

More available books at **www.hansebooks.com**

Zegelda Romanief.

A Story about Music.

By CHARLES BARNARD.

Through darkness riseth light.—The Elijah.

BOSTON:
Musical Herald Company, Music Hall.
1880.

PREFATORY NOTE.

The author would respectfully acknowledge the valuable assistance of Messrs. Hook & Hastings, organ-builders, of Boston, in preparing certain portions of the technical parts of this work.

THE AUTHOR.

New York, September, 1880.

ZEGELDA ROMANIEF.

CHAPTER I.

The harvest now is over, the summer days are gone.—Elijah.

IT was snowing fast, and the dimly-lighted streets of the little town were deserted. Even the shop-keepers thought it useless to keep open on such a bad night, and were already putting up their shutters, though it was only seven o'clock. It was a good night to keep within, a good night to sleep, and it seemed as if the entire community intended to improve the opportunity early. On a wooden fence in Main Street was a single poster, setting forth, in small type, the fact that there would be a "grand concert" that evening at the Music Hall. A sorry night for a concert in a rural town.

The Music Hall was an old church fallen to base uses, and now half opera house, half lecture room. It had a stage and curtain and three sets of dilapidated scenery, and some hundreds of second-hand seats. There was one gas-lamp flaring in a broken lantern over the wooden steps that led up to the battered door, marked with a tin sign "Main Entrance." The snow lay in a winrow on the sidewalk, and not a footstep had broken its shape. To the rear or stage door, on a back street, there came a party of five people, two men, two women, and one child, with one trunk and two hand-bags between them. A boy with a lantern opened the door, and led the way up the crazy stairs to a barn-like room with neither carpet nor fire. On the dingy wall was a single gas-lamp in a wire cage, and in the corner two broken-back chairs. The two men placed the trunk on the floor, and then followed the boy across the dusty stage to the hall. In a corner under the gallery, standing before a big stove, they found the janitor of the hall.

The two women sat down in the wretched dressing-room, one in silent despair, the other with a stolid patience that seemed to care nothing for the unhappy plight which they were in. The child sat on the trunk, and stared at the lamp in its cage on the wall. A strange girl, apparently more than a child, and yet not quite a woman. She was thin and pale as if half-fed and ill-clothed; yet her black eyes seemed to burn with a restless glow, as if she had a brave spirit touched with fire. With all the poverty, privation, and misery of her life, she was happy. She beat time to some melody in her mind on the old trunk with fingers that were thin and long. She seemed to anticipate something. Very soon the lights would be turned up, the people would throng into the place, she would put on her white dress and would sing for them. Unconsciously, her lips parted, and her voice seemed to ripple, in half whisper, half music, a sparkling stream of notes,—a tawny brook flowing through shady woods, and flecked with sunshine.

The elder woman listened to her for a moment, and said aloud,—

"There's a fortune in them notes, some day."

The child's mother smiled in a sickly, almost ghastly manner, and said,—

"So her father has said, but the public seems to care nothing for them. Even her father has lost heart. This last trip has taken all the courage out of him. We never met with such disaster before."

The elder woman actually seemed to snarl at her. "Whose fault is it? I'm sure my husband put up all the capital for the trip. You said there was money in the girl? Where is it now?"

"You said yourself, just now, there was money in her voice."

"I said there would be a fortune in her some day, not now."

The child stopped singing; and her mother shook her head dubiously, and made no reply. Nobody believed in the child, except its mother. Its father had faith in the girl's future at one time, but that time had gone. The room was dark and cold, but for the girl it was nothing. The concert would begin soon. Her father would sit at the piano, and she would catch up the notes, and repeat them with happy ease. What could be more beautiful than to sing?

"Isn't it almost time for me to dress, mother?"

The elder woman laughed in a sneering manner, and the mother said wearily,—

"Wait a little, child. We must see what sort of a house we shall get."

Just then the two men returned, with the janitor of the hall. The child rose at once, for she knew the trunk must be opened to get out their concert dresses. The elder of the two men unlocked the trunk, and took out a well-worn black dress coat.

"If that will settle the bill-poster's claim, you may take it."

The child went to her father, and took his hand. A vague sense of impending trouble filled her heart. Perhaps there would be no concert, after all. The others looked on in stony indifference. This was the end, the bottom round of the ladder. There was nothing more to be done, and it made little difference what became of anything. When a ship is going down, nobody is very particular to save the sails or furniture.

Round and round the country, from town to town, from hall to hall, they had travelled, appearing night after night to smaller and smaller audiences. When they set out, they had seven trunks. This was the last one left. The janitor examined the coat carefully, and said slowly,—

"I guess he will call it square for that, seeing you had so few bills. I guess you have had bad luck, and I'll let the rent go. The last concert company here lost forty dollars, and they had a great deal of printing. Fact is, our folks don't care much for good music. The minstrels showed here last night to $120,— not a woman in the house. I reckon it about dreened the town for this week. It's only a hundred-dollar place, at best."

He helped them with the trunk down the stairs to the street; and then they went away down the steep, slippery street, towards the river, in dull and heart-broken silence. The men carried the trunk between them to the hotel where they had all slept the night before, and the women and child crept slowly after them. They placed the trunk on the hall floor, where they well knew it would remain. It would perhaps settle their bill, and that was the end of it.

There was a brief consultation in the cold and cheerless office, some whispered words with the sleepy clerk, and then the entire party went out into the night, into the snow-blinded street, without baggage, homeless, houseless, and apparently penniless. Before them, just across the way, was the river, black and vast in the night. The wind sighed in the naked trees, but the river was silent, swift, and cold. On either hand, to the right and left, stretched a long row of blinking gas-lamps, marking where the street led away into the open country.

The party was at the end of its resources. They had parted with everything, and could keep up no longer. The manager was the first to take the decisive step. They were reduced to that condition where all cohesion was lost, and the troupe would go to pieces. He spoke to his wife, who had acted the part of the ballad-singer in their concerts, and they both began to move off to the right down the street leading to the open country.

"I dare say we can find a skiff somewhere along the river; and we'll head off the night-boat, and leave these wretches to shift for themselves."

The woman seemed to agree to this, and in a moment they were walking away, leaving the father and mother of the child alone in the street.

The father and the musical leader of the party ran after them for a few steps, and asked where they were going.

"It's none of your business," said the manager. "When it gets down to this, every man looks for himself."

With that, they were gone,—lost in the darkness.

The child began to cry piteously; for the damp snow chilled her feet, and she had neither muff nor gloves.

Suddenly, the mother snatched up the child in her arms, and moved across the street towards the river.

"Where are you going with that child?" said her husband.

"I'm going to mend her misery and mine—or end it."

* * * * * * * *

The captain and pilot both stood by the wheel in the pilot-house, looking out on the storm and darkness. The throb of the engine came slowly and monotonously, and the vast bulk of the steamer moved silently through the black water and invisible snow. The hills on either side were dim ghosts of a phantom country. It was the last trip down, and the few belated travellers had wisely sought their comfortable state-rooms for the night.

Suddenly there was a faint light dancing on the water just ahead, and at the same instant the lookout, on the deck below, sang out,—

"Boat ahead, sir!"

The captain pulled the bell, and the engine stopped. They must go slow on such a night at the slightest hint of danger. The silence of the river, the night, and the falling snow, was appalling. A door opened below, and the second officer came on deck.

"What do you make her out?"

"Small boat, sir. Shows a light. Seems to be in distress."

"Keep her to port a little," said the captain to the pilot. Then he leaned out of the window, and said,—

"Stand by below, with a line to pick her up."

"For heaven's sake, take us aboard!" cried a voice from the water.

The bell rang again, and the engine moved slowly, and white sheets of creamy water swept past the bows, glistening in the steamer's lamps. More men came out on deck. A rope was skilfully thrown and caught, and in a moment the frail, open boat was drawn up alongside.

"That was a crazy trip for a man and woman," said the second officer. "You may be thankful we saw you."

The engine throbbed again, the skiff was cast adrift, and the people hastily sought the shelter of the saloon.

The rescued party found the captain's office, and paid for a state-room for man and wife and two passages to the city. Very few people saw this singular incident, and in the quiet of the night it was soon forgotten.

They sat up in their state-room for a long time, carefully counting a large roll of bills.

"We did pretty well, take it all together."

"Yes; but I still think it would have been better to hang on to the child a little longer. There's more money in her yet,—when her voice is trained."

"Make hay while you can, is my motto," replied the husband.

With this remark, they hid the money in their clothing, and retired for the night.

CHAPTER II.

He that shall endure to the end shall be saved.—Elijah.

THE avenue was thronged with people just returning from afternoon-service. The churches had been well attended, for the day was pleasant, though cloudy; and it was midwinter, when all the fashionable world was in town, busy over its idle nothings, and eager to go to church, hear the music, and be comfortably saved from its various sins. From the doors of St. Clement's came out a multitude that, in its strictly proper way, considered itself representative of the saints on earth in good social standing. If there were sinners among them, they descended from the organ-loft. In the church vestibule, gloomy with stained glass, there was a little buzz of excitement. Such a thing had never happened before. St. Clement's had been scandalized. The very gargoyles on the eaves looked the more ugly than ever to think such doings had been allowed under the sacred roof of which they were such pious servants. Even the plaster angels round the base of the dome had turned pale, and shook the dust from their folded wings in holy horror.

Lovers had sat in the dark corners, and held each other's hands during the sermon. Boy-lovers had passed caramels to little girls, and even baby-sinners· had whispered in prayer-time. These were sins that would doubtless be punished in due time, but they were as nothing to a more blatant crime that had defiled the very air of the church. The larger part of the congregation frowned, and hoped something would be done about it, and then went peacefully home with a comfortable sense of duty done. A few remained behind to see what would happen. They gained but little; for, when the choir came down, they were one by one invited privately into the vestry, there to meet the church-music committee. There was the organist, a tender young thing, lacking in everything save fingers; a rather gorgeous soprano, a timid little alto, a black-whiskered bass, and the tenor. He deserves brief mention. He was young, well-made, though pale and thin, and with a faint suggestion of poverty about his dress; a man of quiet manners and placid temperament; evidently, a man who thought much and said little.

The music-committee was composed of a lawyer who could not read music, a banker who had neither voice nor ear, two merchants who knew nothing of music, and the minister of the church. The minister was really the only man who knew anything whatever about music, and yet they were met to sit in judgment on the choir.

St. Clement's was passing through the barbarous age. In due time would come another and a wiser who would make all things new.

"It appears from good evidence," said the lawyer, "that the music you gave to-day, both at the morning and afternoon service, was not suitable to the time or place."

The banker added that the music, though fitted to a hymn, reminded one of the opera from which it had been taken, and thus led to thoughts very far from those of the hymn.

The minister regretted this had happened, and asked what the choir had to say.

Both ladies were voluble in protesting that they had no choice in the matter. They sang what was placed before them.

"You are ladies, and had a lady's influence. Did you use it?"

Well, no. They sang the music given to them.

The bass singer remarked that he didn't see that it made any difference. Music was music.

"All right," said the lawyer: "you can sing elsewhere."

This brought a wail from the soprano and tears from the alto, though she strove hard to hide them. The organist made some feeble protest, and the bass insisted he should stand by his contract.

"Then you had better read it again," remarked the banker.

The tenor said nothing. He had protested at the rehearsal, the night before, against the use of the music, yet he would not take an advantage over his co-laborers. It was better to suffer an injustice than to do an unkindness.

The contract between the choir had been carefully drawn, and, by one of its sections, such an offence as this dissolved it instantly.

"You will please call at my office to-morrow," said the banker, "for your pay up to date. You have permission to withdraw."

The five went out in silence; and the janitor, with a grin of ill-disguised malice, closed the doors of the church upon these miserable sinners cast out into outer darkness.

It was indeed outer darkness, for the night and a storm had come. As they gathered in the deserted street, by the light of a gas lamp, the soprano gave the organist a rather acrid piece of her mind; and, like the small creature that he was, he turned and stung her with the remark that the particular piece of music that had made all the trouble had been sung at her request. The little alto was in tears. Poor child! Her lines were hard. The pay from the church was absolutely her only means of support; and now she was thrown out of it, and through no fault of her own.

"See what your stupidity has brought us to!" said the bass, shaking his fist at the organist. "I've half a mind to thrash you."

"Oh! Come now, gentlemen," remonstrated the tenor, "let us have no scene in the street. It won't help the matter in the least. I dare say we can all find new places."

For the moment, the organist made no reply. It was afterward reported he said many bitter and ill-natured things against the whole choir. Rumor also has it that for this he was privately thrashed by the soprano's husband. It is to be hoped that this last was true.

There was nothing more to be said or done; and the organist, bass, soprano, and alto went their several ways in silence, leaving the tenor alone in the walk, in the shadow of the great church.

Here is a point in human experience,— a mere episode in art-life and apparently trifling, but really wide-reaching in its influence, and affecting one life, at least, for all time. We strive and do and bear, and life moves on, and our doings and strivings bear strange fruits. Even our burdens sometimes blossom with unexpected flowers.

"If you please, sir, could you give me something to get a night's lodging?"

The tenor turned to see who spoke, and found a child, thinly and poorly clad, and with a scared and starved look in her eyes, at his side. Begging was the curse of the city; and he was on the point of turning away in disgust and anger, when a woman advanced into the circle of light under the street lamp, and said quickly,—

"I must ask pardon, sir, for the child; but the fact is we are actually suffering for food and shelter."

The young man felt in his pocket for a coin,

and then remembered that he was almost as poor as they.

"I know nothing about you," said he; "but the child seems to be really suffering."

"Father was killed some time ago, when we were walking on the railroad."

"We buried him, sir," added the woman, "in the town where we were, in a pauper's grave; and then we two travelled on to the city. We have neither friends nor home nor money."

"I live with a woman who is a milliner. She has a spare room. I'll borrow it for you for to-night. Perhaps it will be a fairer day to-morrow for us all."

"I knew he would help us," said the child. "And, mother, he speaks in song words. He means it will not snow, and we shall find help to-morrow."

The young man drew her to the light, and looked into her upturned face for a moment in silence.

"Child, you have the art instinct. I'll be your friend. Come, let us go home."

Is charity always wise? In the case of the young man taking the strange woman and her child to his home, it seemed like charity without reason and altogether foolish. Whether it was wise or foolish, events must prove. His landlady considered the affair almost an affront. The woman and child were total strangers. Why should she admit them to her house? She listened to their story; and, though her sympathy was touched, she was unwilling to take them in till her lodger had said he would be responsible for them, and even then, after assigning them a room next his own, carefully locked up the rest of the house against them.

The morning broke late and cloudy; and the young man rose before daylight, and, having made a cup of coffee by a gas-stove, and eaten a loaf of bread left by the baker at the door, he sat down to examine the situation.

To understand all that passed in his mind, we must glance at the events of his previous life. Born upon a farm in Illinois, Sebastian Strove had, until he was sixteen years of age, known little of life except its toil. His father had emigrated from Norway when quite young, and had, by a life of labor, secured a home and farm and family. During his whole life in this country, his range of thought had just about covered the farm, and no more. Upon his farm and crops, he had spent his life. The result was admirable in nearly every sense. If he had failed in any sense, time would show it in his children's lives. He had married young, and there were many children,— good, commonplace boys and girls, of no special interest to any one except their parents, save one, the eldest born, who had taken his father's name, Sebastian.

While his father's antecedents were clear, his mother's history, previous to her marriage, was somewhat obscure. She had come to the Illinois township from Worcester, Massachusetts. At least, she said so; and Western hospitality, that seldom asks who the visitor is, but only what he or she can do, had been extended to her on every side. She had sufficient money to pay her way, and was a quiet and retiring young woman, able and willing to work and maintain her own place in society. She was well educated, could sing, and, it was said, could play the piano. This last could not be proved, for the reason that there was no piano in the town. She readily found her niche in society as the village schoolmistress, but it was not for long. She received several offers of marriage, including one from the rising young Norwegian, Sebastian Strove; and, after some delay, she had accepted him.

The farm was then little more than rough soil; the homestead, a log cabin. The farmer's heart was set on improving both; and his wife proved, indeed, a helpmeet. He was greatly pleased with her housewifely ways, and he gave her as much of his heart as could be spared from the farm.

For the wife, the log cabin was a safe haven of rest, a secure shelter from the terrible storm that had passed over her young life. She cared only for peace and forgetfulness, a hiding-place from all who had known her in distant Massachusetts. She was a silent woman, doing her whole duty to her husband and children, and loving them all, particularly the eldest born boy, whom she regarded with a kind of blind, unreasoning passion.

Other children came in time; but, for some reason, she never seemed to care for them as for the eldest born. He was unlike his brothers or sisters either in looks or temperament. He was from his boyhood a dreamer and idler, a strange child, who loved to roam abroad over the flat, unlovely fields, silent and alone, or with a stick in hand beating time to some wild melodies he sang or whistled. The mother saw him grow up, first with fear, then with admiration. He had the face and manner of one whom she wished to forget and could never forget. Sometimes a tone in the child's voice, an expression on his face, startled her. It was so like one whom she should hate and once did love. For the father, the boy was a sore vexation and trial. He would not work except on compulsion, and this was a grievous sin. The other boys were good enough, and would go for the cows or help in the field. The eldest boy was an idler, a disgrace to his father's name. He had been to school; but he made no progress there, and he was taken back to the farm. His mother had wished him to stay longer at school, but his father objected. His mother then began to teach him herself in secret; and at last, seeing the passionate love of his wife for the boy, he had consented that she might teach him one day every week. Other children had come; but, for some reason, she never gave them the special education she bestowed on him. So it happened that, in time, he was much better educated than his brothers and sisters. Among other things, she had taught him all she knew of music.

In time, the mother's instruction bore unexpected fruit. The boy became more of a reader than worker, more of student than farmer. He loved more to wander through the scanty timber in the intervale, to sing in the village choir, than to work on the farm. His father complained bitterly of what he called his idleness, but his mother always took his part. At last, the difference between himself and father concerning his labor on the farm had grown so serious that, with the secret assistance of his mother, he had run away from home, and had arrived, two years since, alone and almost penniless in the city.

By good luck, his pleasant voice and readiness to please all he met won him a place in a church choir. The church had employed his time only one day in the week; and the salary, by the aid of the most rigid economy, kept him from want. He might have spent the remaining six days in some other employment; but he chose rather to earn less and learn more. He sang on the Sabbath, and spent the week-days in study. First, he had tried, as best he could, to repair his general education by reading; and at the Public Library he found the right tools, books. Secondly, he studied music, and particularly church music. He went as often as the chance offered to week-day services, he heard all the organs possible. He read and actually sang through (for he often had no piano) all the books of church music he could beg or borrow. His dream was to discover or create something better, something more effective, more artistic, than the ordinary church music he heard in the Protestant churches of the city. He had even gone so far as to map out an ideal church choir.

With all this, the actual outcome of his life seemed to be only want and failure. He had gained a footing in a good and well-paid choir; but he had made many changes, and once was out of work for a whole month, which nearly reduced him to beggary. With all this, he had faith in himself, and felt sure he would one day succeed. He had thought he might, perhaps, teach music. Some persons made a good deal of money by teaching; but a brief trial with one poor pupil, who could not pay anything, convinced him that he had no gift in that direction. The position in the choir at St. Clement's had supported him with difficulty; and now it was gone, and through no fault of his own. He looked about the bare little room, with its faded carpet and well-worn furniture, and wondered if all his life was to be passed in such poor quarters. Suddenly there seemed to be on the air a faint hint of music. Then there was silence for a moment. Then it came again, louder and clearer,— a pure though childish soprano, fluttering from note to note, like a bird trying its wings for a bolder flight. Then it ran quickly up the scale for two full octaves, and back again, in confident ease and precision. It was the child in the next room.

A moment after, there was a timid knock at the door, and the child herself looked in.

Sebastian bid her enter; and she came into the room, and stood looking at him curiously. Then she seemed to gain confidence, for she came nearer and said,—

"Mother sent me to thank you, sir, for the night's shelter. I don't know what we could have done without your help."

"Oh, never mind! You have paid me already."

"Paid you, sir?"

"Yes,— by singing

"Oh! you heard me in the next room. I always sing when I am happy. The birds do so. I suppose they must be always happy."

"Have you been to breakfast?"

"Yes: the woman downstairs called us early, and gave us a good breakfast. I think all I need now is a piano."

"The landlady has a piano downstairs. She lets me use it at night."

"Night is a good way off."

"Yes; but in the day-time she uses the room for her business."

"Oh!" said the child, with a look of pleased curiosity. "You play the piano? Perhaps you sing, also. I knew by your face you were Romany."

"Romany! What's that?"

"Gypsy. I am Romany. My name is Zegelda."

"Oh, I'm not a gypsy at all. My name is Sebastian Strove. I am an American. My mother came from Massachusetts. My father was a Norwegian."

"That makes no difference. You have the Romany look in your eyes. You love music. We all do,— we Romany folk."

The child had come nearer to him, and stood by his side, with evident pleasure. She was pale and thin, and yet very beautiful. She seemed to be quite young, and yet with her youth there was just a hint of approaching maidenhood. Her eyes were dark and luminous, and her hair long and deep black. She laid one hand on his arm, and the touch seemed to thrill him. It was a clinging touch, as if she looked to him for protection. In all his life, he had never seen so much of girlish beauty and confidence.

"I shall like you."

"I am glad to know it," he replied, and was

at once surprised that he should have said so. "Tell me more about yourself. Where did you come from? Who were your father and mother?"

"My father was Romany. His name was Romanief. He came to this country long since, and settled — in that Eastern State with the long name. You said it just now."

"Massachusetts?"

"Yes, it was Massachusetts. In a town they called — I forget it now. I shall remember it presently. He taught music there. He had much of your looks. He was an artist, a great singer, though those cold and stupid Eastern people knew it not. Then he travelled out West, and married my mother; and they sing in concerts, and teach music. I, too, sing in concerts, till we grew very poor. At last, we were so poor we travel from town to town on foot. It was thus he was killed on the railroad. Ah! now I recall the place where he once lived. It was Worcester, Massachusetts."

CHAPTER IV.

Be not afraid.—Elijah.

THE musical life has always been the subject of both praise and blame. To many persons, the peculiar emotional temperament that marks the musician seems admirable. For others, the musical life appears strange, unreal, and unpractical, a kind of emotional craze, ruinous to business and quite incompatible with a good bank account.

In Sebastian Strove, the farmer lad from Illinois, appears one phase of the musical life. He stands for the newer art-life of this country,—enthusiastic, earnest, and yet intensely and really practical. Willing to sacrifice ease and money to attain his end, which is musical culture; apparently unthrifty and thoughtless of the future, and yet looking beyond the near future to that farther future, where he sees greater rewards in art.

Zegelda is a type of the older musical temperament,—very emotional, intensely egotistical, easily moved, and careless of everything save music. Having made each other's acquaintance, they seemed to readily understand each other's hopes and aspirations. They both wished to live the musical life. To illustrate her character, we may notice that neither she nor her mother knew where they were to sleep that night, nor were they positive as to their next meal, and yet she said,—

"I think all I now need is a piano."

Sebastian had heard the reference to Worcester, his mother's former home, with surprise. Could there be any possible connection between this girl's father and his mother? The thought passed through his mind, but he dismissed it at once. For the girl there was, of course, nothing remarkable in the fact. She knew nothing of Sebastian's family history; and yet this mere mention of the town was the little cloud that, like as a man's hand, had risen above their horizon.

There was no piano in the house except in the landlady's parlor; and, as that room was used in the day-time in her millinery business, it could not be opened.

"If you will put on your things, we will go down town, and see if we can find a piano."

"Then you must be rich. I'm glad of it, for I really need a piano."

"Rich! Oh, no! Far from it. I'm quite poor. I had a good place yesterday, but I lost it."

The girl looked at him with wide-open eyes, and said seriously,—

"I knew you were Romany. Never mind, your luck will turn to-day. I will put on my things at once."

With that she disappeared. What a singular child,— no, woman! She was a woman a child-woman. In spite of his matter-of-fact training, he smiled to himself. What if his luck should change! It had been running the wrong way a long time.

"Pshaw! There's no such thing as luck."

Yet luck was at the door, for just then the girl returned. Her well-worn cloak and hat seemed transformed, and she really looked quite presentable. She came in with a light, half-dancing step, and with shining eyes and a bright smile.

"This house is lucky. The woman down-stairs gave my mother seventy-five cents to work for her to-day, making bows for hats. We shall now have a good dinner. Perhaps you will dine with us. She also gave me a piece of ribbon, and I pinned it into my hat. Is it not pretty?"

She stood looking at him, and all the while turning her head this way and that in a bird-like fashion, and softly singing to her self. What a wonderful voice she had! It seemed to Sebastian to thrill him, just as the touch of her hand on his arm had done.

His silence seemed to trouble her, and she stopped singing and said gravely,—

"Are you offended, sir? Perhaps it was wrong for mother to ask for work."

"No, I'm not offended. I am glad she has found something to do. I was thinking of your voice."

"I have a good voice, and I mean to make a great singer. I have sung in concerts often."

This she said with straightforward simplicity, as if it was the most natural thing in the world.

"Did you ever sing in church?"

"No. I should not wish to. It's so dark in churches, and the people — they look so unhappy."

The young man laughed at this commentary, and said simply,—

"I fear you do not know much about it. Come, let us go and find a piano."

It is doubtful if the young man knew exactly what he intended to do. He had a vague idea that he might hire a piano for the girl. His income was just nothing a day. To hire even the cheapest piano would necessitate the payment of cartage, if not advance payment of the rent; and his total assets were barely sufficient to support him a month. Of course, a few moments' reflection showed him he could not hire a piano. Besides, where could it be sent? The child had no roof over her head, much less room for a piano. With all this, he steadily kept in view the fact that the girl had something of the art-life in her, and that he would help her as far as it lay in his power.

Zegelda walked on beside him through the streets, in happy confidence. What he intended to do she did not know, but she felt confident that, in some way, he would find a piano for her. Presently they entered one of the principal avenues of the city, and came to an elegant establishment for the sale of pianos. Through the plate glass windows could be seen a number of costly upright pianos.

"Oh, how beautiful! If I had a piano like one of those, I should care for nothing else in the world."

"Let us go in," said Sebastian. "I wish to see some of the people here. I will not keep you waiting long."

The girl entered the warerooms timidly, and advanced towards a piano in an ebonized case, rich with carvings of birds and flowers. She paused in silent admiration before it, forgetful of everything about her. She had never seen anything so splendid, and yet it seemed quite proper. Anything that had to do with music should be beautiful. She walked about it, looked at it from every side, and even touched the keys with one hand in a soft, caressing manner. The piano seemed to whisper as if it dreamed. The sound appeared to have no tangible quality, but to be only a shadow of music,— an echo of harmony, as if the dumb instrument recognized its mistress.

When Sebastian entered the store, he left Zegelda by the door, intending, himself to go to the counting-room at the rear of the place, and ask for the loan of one of the rooms provided by the firm for the use of musical people. There were several rooms in the upper part of the building, each warmed and provided with a piano; and it was Sebastian's intention to obtain one of these rooms, and to take the girl there and try her voice, and see if by its use anything could be done for her support. This intention, while it may serve to show his thoughtful and practical character, he did not carry out.

In passing through the long wareroom, he came upon a party of four gentlemen earnestly talking together. One of them he remembered as an agent for professional singers. This person, Mr. Sill by name, had an office in the city, where he kept a list of singers, choirs, and concert companies; and it was his self-elected mission in the musical world to act as a go-between among these parties. He found singers for choirs and business for concert troops, and even dabbled in concerts himself, by which speculative ventures he generally managed to burn everybody's fingers but his own. Sebastian, on his first arrival in the city, had been led by an advertisement to apply to him, and had even paid him ten dollars for assistance in finding a place in some choir, which assistance, as was his custom, the said Sill had never rendered. Personally, the creature was short and fat, with a partially bald head, and with small gray eyes and a stubby red moustache. His whole make-up was repulsive and disagreeable, and Sebastian had intended to pass him by without notice; but the man saw him, and came hastily toward him, and said in a whisper,—

"Morning, sir. Would you like a place at St. Clement's?"

"Thank you, I left there only yesterday."

"Oh, yes, I forgot. I think I got you the place at first. Well, they made a clean sweep of it; and now they have formed a new choir, all but the tenor. If you will give me ten per cent. of the salary for the first three months, I'll get you the place."

"They turned me out with the rest. It is useless to think they would take me back."

"Yes, they will, if I say so. They know me. I'll answer for you. It will be only ten per cent."

"I've paid you ten dollars already, and you never brought me a single opening."

"Oh, yes, I forgot! I will call that on account. I was thinking I did something for you."

With that, he moved away toward the group of gentlemen. After a brief consultation, the business was settled. Sebastian explained that he was not in any way to blame for the music of the day before. A memoranda of agreement was drawn up, and it really seemed as if, as the girl had said, his luck had turned. Just as Sebastian was about to sign the paper, there seemed to be on the air a pure and beautiful note, sustained by almost unheard harmony from a piano. One of the elder gentlemen looked over his glasses toward the door in surprise. Mr. Sill was for a moment startled, but pretended indifference. Immediately after the business was settled, the gentleman who had listened to the voice from the piano moved toward the door. Sebastian looked about, and noticed that other people seemed to have been listening; and he was in momentary alarm lest Zegelda would sing again, and attract farther attention to herself. Not that he was ashamed to have brought her there, but he felt instinctively that she was impulsive and thoughtless, and that she might commit some breach of propriety in this rather severe and elegant place. He bid the gentlemen good-morning, and moved toward the door, only to find that the agent was following him.

"You ought to make it twenty per cent.; for the place is a good one, and you are sure to keep it."

"You said your terms were ten per cent. I will give you that, less the ten dollars, at the end of the first quarter."

"You couldn't make a little advance now? I'm very short to-day."

The fact that the man had a well-filled purse made no difference. It was his instinct to plunder wherever he thought he could.

"No, sir, I have no money to-day. You must wait till I earn something."

By this time, they had advanced to the front of the wareroom. Mr. Sill made a note in his memoranda, and passed out into the street without noticing Zegelda, who stood by the piano. She drew near to Sebastian, and he observed that she was pale and trembling with excitement. Her black eyes seemed to blaze with passionate anger after the retreating form of the agent on the walk outside.

"Do you know him?"

"Why, yes. It is Mr. Sill, the musical agent."

"I know him. He is not always called Sill. He goes by other names at times. I hate him."

"Hate him! Why, what has he done to you? Where did you ever meet him?"

"I hate him — it is enough — I hate him."

The girl's passionate outbreak against the musical agent was an unpleasant surprise to Sebastian. It was a new revelation of her character; and he moved toward the street door without making any comment on her invective, and said quietly that they must go. Without a word, she followed him into the street, and walked on by his side in silence. What could he do with the girl? He could not ask for the use of a room and piano after such an episode in the warerooms. He began to feel that perhaps he had made a mistake. Why should he trouble himself about this strange girl? Perhaps, after all, she was not worthy any special pains. His financial affairs were certainly improved, he was better able to help her, and yet he felt inclined to shake her off, and let her take care of herself as best she might.

Just then he felt her arm steal into his, and rest there confidingly. He turned to look at her, and saw a tear trembling on her cheek.

"O sir, you are angry with me! I am very sorry."

"No: I am not angry,— only sorry you should have spoken so rudely of Mr. Sill in the warerooms."

"His name is not Sill. He is a thief. He robbed my father, and I hate him. I shall tell you about him some time — not now."

He made no reply to this, and they walked on for some moments in silence. She still kept his arm, and seemed to cling to him for protection. At first, he was annoyed. Had she been a girl near his own age, he would have dropped her arm and resented the familiarity. She was only a child, and he could not resist the impulse to draw her arm closer within his own.

"You will forgive me, sir, will you not?"

"Why, certainly. It's of no consequence now."

"Oh, I am very glad!" she said gayly. "And now, if you please, I think I should have a piano. I will be very sweet and good, if you will get one."

The abrupt change in her manner, from tearful entreaty to merry banter, was another revelation. Could it be she was utterly shallow and thoughtless, or was there more below this shifting surface?

"I really ought not to miss my practice hour."

"You are right: you must practise every day. So must I, for it is the only road to success in music. I meant to have asked for the use of a piano at the warerooms; but I met some gentlemen who made me an offer to sing in church, and the business put the piano quite out of my mind."

"Do you get much money for singing in church?"

"The salary is very good."

"I told you good luck would come to-day."

"I hope so. My luck has been against me so far."

"Never mind, sir. It will change after this. I feel sure of it."

There must be something of the gypsy in the girl. Her mobile face, constantly varying in expression; her gayety and lightness of manner; her ready tears, almost dropping amid her laughter, — puzzled and yet charmed him. It was a new and delicious sensation to have her by his side. The busy street and gay shops appeared to excite her, and she talked rapidly and in happy ease, as if she had known him all her life, and as if the problem of obtaining the next meal and that night's lodging had no existence. He explained to her that he had intended to borrow the use of a piano and try her voice, but that the business had prevented, and that after dinner he would see what could be done about it.

"Yes: I suppose I must have a dinner. I hope the woman who gave mother the work will pay her something by noon; for we haven't a cent in the world."

"You shall dine with me," said Sebastian, in a sudden burst of generosity. "Here's a good restaurant. Let us go in."

"Thank you, sir: you are very kind. We might have some oysters and half a chicken and some cream."

The proposal nearly took his breath away. Such a bill of fare would cost more than ten meals at home. Yet he led her into the restaurant and took seats, and actually began to write an order for oysters, spring chicken, and ice-cream, when she laid her hand on his arm, and said gravely,—

"Perhaps the oysters and chicken might not agree with me. Let us order a steak. It will be enough for two."

Was she child or woman, gypsy sprite or sober New England maiden with more sense than common? The steak was ample for them both; and she said she really did not care for the cream, so the order was not given. For the young man, brought up in the hard life of a Western farm, unfamiliar with the art temperament, and still less familiar with young feminine society, the little dinner was a royal feast, the most delightful meal he had ever eaten.

He was as good as his word, and that afternoon took her to another piano warehouse, where he obtained the use of a piano and room for an hour. Zegelda sang for him for some time, while he listened in silence. She asked what he thought of her voice, but he put her off with vague compliments, that seemed to satisfy her completely. Then they went home, Sebastian talking but little and letting her chatter on rather idly. He had made a discovery, perhaps two. He must think about it.

Luck really seemed to have come to the house. Zegelda's mother had so far satisfied the milliner that she had given her a week's work, and had offered her and the child a home in her house, and had even made a small cash payment in advance. The practising question was also arranged by allowing Zegelda the use of the piano in the night; and, by sitting up late and rising late in the morning, five hours' practice could be secured without injury to her health.

On the following Saturday, Sebastian went to the rehearsal at St. Clement's, and so far pleased the new organist and director that they welcomed him as a valuable addition to the choir. At ten o'clock, Sunday morning, while in his room, preparing to go to the church, there came a knock at his door; and, thinking it might be the landlady, he bid her come in.

It was a young woman, neatly, almost handsomely, dressed in some dark stuff that was wonderfully becoming. He looked at her in surprise for a moment; and then her grave and handsome face broke into smiles, and with a laugh she bowed, and said,—

"Miss Romanief — at your service, sir. And please, sir, may I go to church with you? I never went to church in my life."

"Never went to church, Zegelda?"

"Well, yes, I've looked in once or twice with mother. Father did not wish me to go to church. It seemed so dark and sad, and the people looked very unhappy. Perhaps it would be different, if I went with you."

Then she came nearer, and said with childlike simplicity,—

"The landlady gave me the material,— it's one of her old dresses,— and I made it up myself. Isn't it very pretty? Mother made the hat for me."

"They are both very pretty, but the dress makes you look like a woman."

"I am a woman," she said gravely, as if it was an important fact. Then she changed her manner in an instant, and said: "You are not polite. You should say, 'Mr. Sebastian Strove will be greatly pleased with Miss Romanief's company at church.'"

"I will. I shall be ready in five minutes, and call for you."

"Miss Romanief presents her compliments to Mr. Strove, and will accept his kind invitation with pleasure." Then, with a rippling laugh, she swept out of the room, and in a moment a glorious voice made the cheap and dingy lodging-house re-echo with *bravura* cadenzas.

The young man pulled on his well-worn gloves, and muttered to himself that things were getting dangerous. She was not a child at all; or, if a child, she was just stepping into a beautiful maidenhood before his eyes. The wan, pinched face of the girl of a week ago seemed to belong to some long-distant past. This was another Zegelda,— a young woman of almost boundless talent, that seemed to hint at undiscovered possibilities in the future. What had he to do with such a being?

She walked gravely by his side on the way to church, among a throng of fashionable people, as self-possessed, as ladylike, and more beautiful than any of them. People turned to look after the tall, lank youth, in well-worn suit, and the beauty beside him. He was aware of the admiration the passers bestowed upon her. Had he heard their remarks about her and about himself, he might have wondered greatly. At first, he was jealous of the admiration she evidently won. Yet she was only his child-ward, a poor girl who had needed and claimed his help,— merely a beggar waif from the street.

As they drew near the church, Zegelda glanced up at the Gothic steeple, rich in stone foliage, that seemed to grow from bud to flower, till it blossomed into a cross at the top.

"Why do churches have steeples?"

The question, coming from such a child,

startled him, and for a moment he was at a loss for an answer.

"I really don't know, unless it be to lead the people's thoughts to heaven."

"I think it must be that; for it is like poetry. It is odd that men should think to put a song into stone."

There was a great multitude about the doors of the church, and they found some difficulty in entering the Gothic porch. They pressed through the throng, and in a moment stood within the church, in the dim light, the soft, warm air, and with the lofty roof spread out in dusky arches over their heads.

"How beautiful!"

"Hush! Do not speak so loud!" said Sebastian, with just a shade of annoyance. Some of the people turned to see who thus spoke out in admiration, and perhaps they lingered a moment after to look at the child's strange beauty. Sebastian spoke to an usher near by.

"Will you please find a seat for this young lady? I must go upstairs myself."

"Yes, sir; but not now. The regular attendants must be provided with seats first. Let the lady wait a moment."

"Will you please wait here, Zegelda, till the usher finds you a seat? I must go upstairs, and after church I'll meet you at the door."

"No, no! I want to go with you. Take me with you to the stage — I mean the place where you sing."

Sebastian bit his lip with vexation. She was a perfect child. How could he make her understand that she could not sit in the choir? He led her back into the vestibule, not knowing what to do.

"I am musical. Why should I not sit with the singers?"

"I am afraid they will not permit it."

"Then I must go home. I want to sit with you. I will be very good."

She said this in a childlike, beseeching manner, that was not to be resisted. Just then the organ began, and he knew it was time for him to take his place in the choir. He led her upstairs, and at the entrance of the organ-loft he met the gentleman who sang bass in the choir, and who was also the new director of the music.

"May I take this young lady into the choir with me? She is a stranger here, and does not wish to sit alone."

"Oh, certainly. Bring her in. Your sister, I presume."

"Oh, no! Only a friend."

"Indeed! She's the image of you, except in color. You would pass for brother and sister anywhere."

The speech was rather startling; but, in the confusion of entering the choir and finding a seat for Zegelda,— who seemed to be quite bewildered by the surroundings,— it passed without notice. The place was much like other organ-lofts,— a narrow gallery at the end of the church, with the organ behind and a low railing, with heavy crimson curtains, in front. There were three people there,— two ladies, and, behind them, at the desk, the organist. Zegelda was given a seat next Sebastian's, at the left of the choir. There were also a number of unoccupied seats behind her.

For this child,— all her life roughly knocked about the world, accustomed to want, to perpetual change and travel, familiar only with the life of a travelling show-man, and having a sensitive and artistic temperament, not wholly blunted by poverty,— the place, and, above all, the music from the organ, was a revelation, an unspeakable delight and wonder. Her eyes wandered from the organ to the pointed roof, the stained windows glowing with living color in the bright sunlight, the peaceful angels looking calmly down from the bases of the springing arches, the vast throng of people below and around her. Everything was new and strange; and she thought the people must love music to put it in such a beautiful house. Oh, if she could sing in such a place as this, and with Sebastian! Already her thoughts seemed to turn to him in connection with her life and music.

At the end of the voluntary, the choir stood up to sing. Zegelda's seat was a little in advance of the others; and, when Sebastian stood up with the others, he was directly by her side, as she sat hidden behind the crimson curtains.

As for the young man, he knew that this was a kind of trial for him. If he pleased the people, all would be well. He must do his best. He laid the music-book on the rack before him, and stood up with the others, with his left hand hanging by his side. The anthem began, and went on easily; for it was not difficult. The difficulties were ahead, in the tenor solo, evidently selected to try his voice and style. Suddenly, he felt a small hand placed in his. He glanced down, to see Zegelda looking up at him with beaming eyes, and holding his hand in hers. It was an encouragement. He must do his best for her sake.

Now comes the solo. He took it up confidently. Perhaps something of the child's wonderful spirit came to him through her clinging fingers. He felt he was doing well. There was a profound hush over all the people, as if they had caught the new voice.

"*The Lord is in his holy temple.*"

Suddenly, the clasping fingers tightened on his; and she pressed close to his side, as if for protection. The hand-clasp seemed to be full of passionate appeal for aid and comfort. He glanced down at her face. It was white with alarm and terror. What had happened? Was she ill? Tears stood in her eyes, that seemed frozen as if in agony. He glanced back, and there, on the steps leading down into the choir, sat — squatting like a toad — the agent, Sill.

The voice faltered for an instant. Everything was lost. He would break down. Suddenly there was a meaning pressure on his hand. The pale face looking up at him had a wan and haggard smile. He was safe. It was her spirit in the music.

"FOR THE LORD IS IN HIS HOLY TEMPLE. LET ALL THE EARTH KEEP SILENCE."

CHAPTER V.

Lift thine eyes unto the mountains, from whence cometh help.— ELIJAH.

THE young man finished his work, and sat down. It had been performed without apparent accident, yet he felt sure it was a failure. He had not produced the effect on the people he had intended. The time and place forbidding any sign or demonstration of any kind, the people assumed a decorous calm, and gave their attention to the sermon that followed the music. For all that, their decision had been reached: the young man was not wanted in that church. Conscious in their own virtue, and knowing nothing of the scene that had been enacted in the choir, they decided that the new voice did not suit, and that was an end of the matter. On the morrow, or perhaps after church, the committee who had the matter in charge would inform the singer that his services were no longer needed. The fact that he had already sung in the choir before, they seemed to forget, and, certainly, it made no difference in their opinion concerning him.

As he sat down, Sebastian glanced round to see if the agent was still there, and felt relieved to find he had disappeared. The mystery of the man's movement, the child's uncontrollable terror in his presence, and the dark hints she had thrown out concerning her past relations with him, combined to make the young man apprehensive both for himself and for Zegelda. Her silent appeal to him while he was singing had almost been the cause of a total break-down in the music. As it was, he had with difficulty saved himself; and any defects that had appeared in his performance he attributed to her interruption. He felt sure he had not done his best, and was half-inclined to blame her for it.

Then the end came, and the people prepared

to go home. The organist was busy over his instrument, and said not a word. The other members of the choir talked in whispers together, and suffered their co-laborer to depart without a word or sign of recognition.

It would seem as if the practice of so beautiful an art as music would make people sweeter, more charitable, and better. It does not always, for the reason that many who think they love it really only admire it, and use it as a means to gratify their vanity. They use the fine language of the emotions as a mask. Their music seems the expression of beautiful thoughts, whereas their own hearts are full of envy and all uncharitableness. These people had recognized that the new voice was one of unusual excellence, and yet they were secretly glad he had failed. At the porch the committee on music met the soprano singer and asked her how she liked the tenor.

"Well, there are tenors and tenors. Mr. Sebastian is one of the tenors."

She said this in a pronounced and pert manner, the committee thought infinitely becoming.

"Good quality? . Oh, yes, good enough; but no method, sir, no method,— absolutely no method. Quite wanting in style,— I may say he has no style, no style whatever. He will never do in the world. Your people want more style, more vigor, more dash,— as the French say, he should be more *spiritulle.*"

The young lady's rather astounding French made a deep impression; and the committee were on the point of saying that the new tenor should be dismissed at once, and a singer of more dash and spirit should be engaged in his place, when an elderly person in black silk stepped up and said quietly,—

"If the young man who sang in the choir to-day is not retained, I shall withdraw my subscription to the church and sell my pew. He was the only member of the old choir who was of any use, and he must remain with us."

The soprano turned to see who spoke, and found Miss Tabatha Brown, a maiden lady of mature years, standing before the committee.

Miss Tabatha Brown was a person to be feared in the church. She was a lady of enormous wealth, and rather uncertain temper. It was she who had contributed most largely to the building of the church. She had put in the organ at her own expense and did more than her share toward paying the choir. With all this, she seldom or never interfered in any way with the control of the church affairs. Her remark had therefore all the more weight.

The soprano hastened to say that perhaps, on farther trial, the tenor would prove more satisfactory.

"As you say, Miss," continued Miss Brown, in a rather acidulated manner, "the people want a more *spiritulle* singer, and in the young man they had it to perfection. Your French was quite correct, Miss."

There was a mischievous twinkle in the old lady's eye, as she said this; and one of the committee men looked into his hat to keep from laughing. Miss Brown brought him to a sense of his duty by saying sharply,—

"I trust, sir, you will consider my wishes. This young man is a total stranger to me, but I heard him sing, and that's sufficient. I know enough about music to tell a good voice, when I hear it. He must be retained in the choir."

"Then I shall at once resign," said the soprano.

"Very well, my dear," said Miss Brown, with a smile. "You know your own interests best, I presume."

"Every thing shall be as you wish, Miss Brown," said one of the committee. "It would be rather cruel to dismiss the young man. Some of the younger people in the congregation have not liked him, but I dare say they are hasty in their judgment."

"We should never judge of a fellow-being on one trial. It ill becomes us, while Providence gives a lifetime for trial. I have bought the two pews on each side of the choir; and it is my intention to tear them down and enlarge the choir, and make room for a harp, and perhaps a small orchestra with a chorus. There!" she added, with a little laugh, "I have let the cat out of the bag. I didn't mean to tell my plans just yet. However, it will do no harm."

"I fear, Miss Brown, such a scheme will hardly meet the approval of the church. It will be too expensive."

"Nobody asked the church to bear the expense. I will pay for it myself. I built half the church and put in the organ, and pay the largest pew-tax; and I mean to have my way. This young person, whoever he is, must be kept in the choir; and, if I continue to like him, I shall make him director of the music."

Just here a man in livery appeared at the door, and touched his hat to Miss Brown.

"I'm all ready, John. I go at once." With that, she made a sweeping bow to the bewildered choir and committee, and swept out of the church in a manner at once elegant and impressive.

They walked home together in gloomy silence,

Sebastian absorbed in contemplating the miserable end of another effort to get a foothold in the city, Zegelda clearly seeing that trouble of some kind had come, and that in some way she was concerned in it. He had certainly failed. The very people who had welcomed him to the choir, the night before, hardly spoke to him now. The solo had been a dead failure, and Zegelda was to blame for the whole thing. If she had not been there, all would have been well. If she had not interrupted him just then, and thrown him off his balance, nothing serious would have happened. This was the second time she had placed him in an unfortunate position. Why should he trouble himself any more about her? Why not let her go and find her own way in the world?

Just as they reached the house, she said quietly that she was much obliged to him for taking her to church, and that she would like very much to go again some other Sunday.

"I fear I can never take you, Zegelda."

"Why not? Did I do anything wrong?"

"Well, no, not intentionally; but I fear I have lost my place in the choir. They did not like my singing, and I presume to-night they will tell me I need not come again. If you had stayed downstairs, as I wished, it might not have happened."

If he had struck her, he could not have hurt her more.

"Oh, you think I did it! You think I put you out. Oh, it is terrible! You lost the place, and it's all my fault."

They had reached the house, and with a sob she ran up the steps, as if to escape from him. As she could not open the door till he came up with the key, she was obliged to wait for him, and stood sobbing and trembling on the upper step.

"It is all my living," he said rather savagely, "and now I am thrown out of work again. I shall have to give up, after all, and go back to the farm."

"Oh, don't say that! Don't say that! I can

sing. I will sing at concerts and get much money, and you shall have it all. No one was ever good or kind to me before, and yet I spoiled your business. I am very, very sorry."

"Well," said the young man, relenting somewhat, and opening the door for her to enter, "say no more about it. The harm is done: it is useless to cry over it now. Your mother can, no doubt, find something to do, and next week I'll go back to the farm. Music seems to be a failure with me. I have mistaken fancy for talent. It's the old story of the inflated frog. I've been a fool to care for music, and I'll give it all up and go home."

If there is anything that may be confidently looked for, it is the unexpected. Sebastian Strove returned to the church that evening alone. He did not intend to take Zegelda with him; and, in fact, he saw nothing of her after they parted on the door-step at noon, as she remained in her room with her mother. From the events of the morning, he imagined that his fellow-laborers in the choir might receive him rather coldly, and it was best to go alone. His reception was really almost insulting. Not one in the choir paid the slightest attention to him, beyond what was called for by the business of the evening. One of the men pointed out the page in the music-book, and this was all. The two women ignored him completely.

These things are not pleasant to record. It has been thought that music is refining and elevating. This is not so. Music is a mode of expression. While it may express refinement, religion, fine sentiments, and lofty aspirations, it is not any of these, but merely an aid to their expression. It may also serve things that are rude and altogether vulgar. These people used this wonderful mode of expression, and yet they were themselves unlovely and poor in the spirit of good manners. Why such people are found in church choirs can only be explained by the false estimate the church-going public, in so many instances, places upon its music. The demand is for show and display, for mere effect and high coloring, and, in the competition to get these, little has been thought of the people themselves. The demand has been for voices and not singers, performers instead of musicians. The people have misunderstood music, and have fancied that, because it may be the expression of religion and elevated thought, it is in itself religious and elevated.

Events move quickly among the people we have to do with, and we may soon see this whole matter of choir life and choir music in another and a fairer light. The evening service was got through in some half-hearted fashion; and the young man felt sure that this was his last appearance at that church. The fact that he had signed an agreement to sing in the church would probably be of no avail. If he had failed, the church committee would no doubt consider themselves at liberty to break the contract. Such things had been done, he had heard. The service was over and the people going out, and he was on the point of going, when he thought that, at least, he would be polite to them, however rudely they might treat him; and he bowed to them all, and said good-night. The organist bowed and smiled, and said something that was lost in the roar of his organ as he "played the people out." The others neither by look nor word recognized him in any way. It was no matter. It was all of a piece with his life in the city,— an unbroken stream of ill luck, disappointment, and disaster.

He did not even resent their rudeness. He only wondered at it in a vague way, as if it were something quite apart from his life. He had done his duty; and, had not Zegelda interrupted him in the solo, all would have been well. Of course, he could never sing there again; and, not without a sigh of regret at the lost income and opportunity, he turned into the street toward his wretched lodgings, his poverty and despair.

"It's a pretty dream, but it's all over. I know the worst, and I know my duty. I'll go home to my mother, and tell her I have failed. I'll give up music, and go back to"—

"If you please, sir, will you step this way?"

He looked up to see who spoke, and found it was a man in livery.

"Step to the carriage door a moment, sir. Miss Brown wishes to see you."

Who Miss Brown might be, or what any young lady in a carriage might want of him, he could not imagine. The carriage stood by a street lamp in front of the church, and by the aid of the light he saw an elderly lady in black, looking out and holding the door partly open, as if expecting some one. There were many people on the walk, and in the confusion he did not understand what it all meant.

"There must be some mistake, marm"—

"No mistake at all, sir," said the lady, rather sharply. "I have been waiting for you to come out. I wish to see you. Will you please get in the carriage? I will take you to my house, and explain what I want."

The footman opened the door wide, and the lady retreated into the carriage, as if to make room for him to enter.

"It's all right, sir," said the man, quietly. "She wants to see you on a matter of business. Step right in, sir."

The man said this with an air of respect, as if receiving a guest; and Sebastian, not knowing how to refuse, entered the carriage.

Just then the two ladies of the choir came down the church steps.

"I am completely petrified!" exclaimed the soprano. "Miss Brown has taken the new tenor off in her carriage."

The door was closed, and in a second they were rolling swiftly through the streets toward the fashionable end of the city.

"You will excuse me, sir," said the lady, "for taking you off so unceremoniously. My name is Miss Tabatha Brown. You shall know more of me by and by. All I have to say now is that I have often heard you sing in our church; and I have asked you to come to my house, because I may have a favor to ask of you. What is your name, sir?"

"Strove,— Sebastian Strove. I am sure, marm, I shall be glad to be of service."

"Strove! That's Norwegian. You came from the country, I presume?"

"Yes: from Illinois. I have only been in the city about two years."

"So much the better. You have not had time to be spoiled."

Certainly, the entire adventure was most peculiar. The young man hardly knew what to make of it or of his hostess. She asked him a number of questions about his life and musical studies, and he answered simply and directly, which seemed to win her confidence; for she said,—

"I think we shall get on very well together."

Just then the carriage stopped; and the man opened the door, and Miss Brown said to him,—

"Take Mr. Strove to the music-room, John."

This seemed to be an invitation to get out; and the young man did so, and stood upon the walk as if to help the lady out.

"Thank you, sir," she said, stepping lightly down. "I'm not such an old woman that I can't get out of my own carriage. Please go up with the man, and wait for me."

Evidently, Miss Brown was a person who expected to be obeyed. Then came a confused sense of passing into warm, luxurious rooms, rich with pictures and furniture, and at last they came to a curtained door. The servant led the way past the curtain, and Sebastian found himself in a large place, dimly lighted by a single student-lamp on a piano.

It was a large room, lofty and somewhat longer than wide, with hard-wood floor and painted walls. There was a row of windows, closed by blinds on the inside; along one side of the room; and at the end where he stood the floor was covered with a large rug. Near the piano was a small pipe organ, and a harp. The rest of the room was bare, save in one distant corner were gathered together a great number of cane chairs. There were also shelves along the wall, filled with music in sheets and books. The footman offered a seat, and then left the young man alone in the great room. Never had he seen anything more conveniently and splendidly arranged for music. It was evidently at once studio and concert-room. Miss Brown, whoever she might prove to be, was certainly an admirer of music.

"Please be seated Mr. Strove. I wish to talk to you."

The lady had entered the room by the curtained door, in silence; and he hastily looked for a chair to offer her.

"Thank you, sir. I'll sit here. Oh! I forgot. First, I want you to sing to me. Take the piano or organ, whichever you prefer."

With that, she drew a large arm-chair on the rug before the piano, and sat down.

It was an embarrassing situation,— a total

stranger in this rich and apparently eccentric woman's house, and asked to sing in this offhand manner, as if it were the most natural thing in the world!

Fortunately, he was equal to the occasion. She had meant it as a test; and, had he hesitated or pleaded any inability, it is highly probable that this would have been his first and only appearance in that elegant and fashionable music-room. He sat down to the piano, and began a simple song from memory. Something about the touch and sound of the splendid instrument, the hushed room, and perhaps a dim idea that he was, as it were, on trial for his musical life, nerved him to do his best. The song over, Miss Brown said abruptly,—

"Sing something more."

Three times she did this, without a sign of approval or disapproval, praise or blame. When he had finished, she said, in that peculiar tone that he already recognized as meant for polite command,—

"Please be seated near me. I want to talk to you. People say I am a little crazy,"—she said this with a slight laugh,—"crazy over music. It may be so, but it is an innocent craze; but one thing is certain: I am sane enough to take care of my own money. The church where you sang this morning was built chiefly through my exertions, and in large part with my money. If I had any relatives, I suppose they would say that was insane, too. The organ I built entirely at my own expense. In fact, it is mine. I lend it to the church. Now, I am greatly interested in the success of the church, but unfortunately it has not been wholly successful. It is very large and not half-filled. Moreover, the music does not please me at all; and I have decided to take the whole matter into my own hands. I have the consent of the society to supply the music at my own expense, and in such manner as I wish, for two years. The first thing I want is a man like yourself, who can sing and who will help me. For this reason, I asked you to sing for me. I have heard quite a number already, and you are the first who has wholly pleased me."

Sebastian would have thanked her, but she held up her hand as if to warn him, and went on,—

"I want you for a musical director in my choir. Do you think yourself equal to the task?"

"Well — really — Miss Brown, your proposal comes so suddenly, I hardly know what to say. I can at least try, and I can certainly do as I am told."

"That is exactly what I want. I have asked a dozen men if they would accept the place, and not one before you has said he would do as he was told. They all wanted to do what they pleased, not what I liked. I want some one who will do exactly and entirely as I wish. You will not be responsible to any committee, but to me alone. I shall demand your entire services every day, and I will pay you two thousand dollars a year,— at least, for the present. If you prove worth more, you shall have it. Of course, I shall be glad to hear any suggestions you may make in regard to the music, but the final decision must rest with me. My sole aim in this matter is to show what can be done in the finest possible church music, without regard to expense. Our American church music is generally poor, thin, and trifling. It is my hope to be able to make it better — by example."

She went right on talking rapidly and laying out her plans more in detail, and it was some time before Sebastian could say that he would accept Miss Brown's most liberal and flattering offer.

"It's purely business, sir. To-morrow, if you will call at three o'clock, my lawyer will have a contract ready for you to sign. The first thing you must do is to find a soprano, — a great one, — salary not to be considered at all. However, there is no haste. The choir will not be ready for two months, but your duties will begin to-morrow. It will take all that time to get ready for the first Sunday. I shall rely on you to-morrow. Good-night."

Her manner was abrupt, straightforward, and perhaps imperious; and, when she rose and offered her hand, he considered himself dismissed. A maid appeared as by magic at the curtain, and escorted him to the door.

How he reached home he never knew. He ran and walked, and perhaps, in the dark places between the gas-lamps, he skipped in boyish glee. Never had he read in any novel of more wonderful and splendid prospects. Now his dreams of what he could do would be fulfilled. How pleased Zegelda would be with his good fortune! Now she should have a piano and the best teacher money could procure. He must take her some day to Miss Brown's splendid concert-room to sing for her. She was a soprano worth hearing. Why not Zegelda for the soprano? Perhaps her voice, with culture, would be the pearl of great price that all were seeking.

On reaching his lodgings, he knocked on the landlady's door, and asked if Zegelda and her mother were still up.

"Lor, sir! They're gone!"

"Gone! Gone where?"

"I don't know, sir. They had some kind of a quarrel in their room this evening, and about an hour ago Mrs. Romanief came down with the key of her room; and off they goes, bag and baggage —what little they had. Says she, as she went out: 'Here's the rent up to next week. We are going away.' 'And where are you going?' says I. 'It's no matter.' And with that they went right out into the street. The little one was crying, but I could not keep them, nor would they say where they were going, or how long they would stay. They were a strange lot, sir. I never liked them since they came that Sunday night. I shall not be sorry, if they never come back."

CHAPTER V.

Let all that hath life and breath sing to the Lord.

WHENEVER any one attempts to do sincere and honest work in music, he is sure to find a reward. The art always satisfies the artist. His reward may not assume the shape of money; but, for all that, it is a reward,— it satisfies. To our singer, a poor young man studying and following music hitherto alone, and with only the little approval and sympathy his mother had been able to give him, the proposal made to him by the strange lady, who had so abruptly introduced herself and her plans to him the night before, seemed a dream that would melt away in the clear light of day. He hardly dared to go out of doors in the sharp winter's air, lest the dream shrivel up in the cold light of common-sense. She had said that people called her crazy. It might be so. She was probably some rich and eccentric woman with a craze for music, and he would probably never hear from her again.

One fact remained. Zegelda had disappeared. There was no dream about that. Yet, after all, was not her whole appearance, their singular meeting, the mystery of her former life, and her connection with that wretched creature, Sill,— was it not all a phantasy, a strange episode in his lonely life, of no meaning, and soon to be forgotten?

When the woman told him Zegelda and her mother had disappeared, he was conscious of a shock, a sense of surprise and disappointment. In looking at the whole affair by the calmer light of next day, he made a discovery,— he had learned to love the child. No: she was no longer a child, but a woman. In the brief stay she had made under the same roof, she had won his heart. An overwhelming sense of loss, of disappointment and misery, seemed to cover him. She had left him, of her own free will: she had deliberately run away, without sign of explanation or farewell. He would go out of doors, and try to walk off something of the wretchedness and sense of loss he experienced. Perhaps he could find some trace of her at the music-stores. He would even hunt up the agent, Sill, and see if he knew anything of the girl.

As he opened his door, he found a scrap of paper on the floor. He picked it up and opened it. It was merely a bit of yellow wrapping-paper, with something written upon it in pencil:—

"*Mr. Strove, I put you out yesterday in the song, and maid you lose your place. I never can be any good to you: I am sorry. Good-bye, Zegelda.*"

Poor little misspelled, badly written scrawl, yet he kissed it, and then carefully put it away in his trunk; and, if just a tear or two filled his eyes, they were nothing to his discredit. She had run away because she feared she had done him some harm. She must have fancied she was a burden to him, a hindrance in his progress in life and in music. Now he felt sure he loved her. He must find her, if it took every cent he could earn. He must bring her back, tell her of his great good fortune, and — yes — he would some day marry her, and share it with her. The woman might be crazy about music, but she would hardly be so cruel as to offer him employment, unless she really meant it.

He procured a simple breakfast at a cheap restaurant. He must economize now; for every dollar would be needed for his new mission to find Zegelda, and to win her back to his care and his home. This over, he went out in the direction of the church, in the vague hope that he might meet her, or even Mr. Sill, in the street. As he drew near the church, he saw a team drawn up at the door, and a number of men unloading tools and lumber. On the wagon was the sign of a well-known firm of organ-builders in the city. To his surprise, he found the door of the church open; and, stepping inside, he found a man on guard, who said no one was to be admitted except on business.

"That's Miss Brown's orders, and she's the boss here now."

"Is Miss Brown here?"

"Yes, sir. She's inside, with the architect and the organ-builder."

After a brief talk, the man permitted Sebastian to pass, and he entered the church. All the pews and the pulpit were draped in cloths, and the windows were open to give plenty of light. In a pew near the centre of the house sat Miss Brown, and beside her stood two gentlemen. The moment she saw him she smiled and beckoned to him. He went to her, when, to his surprise, she presented him to the organ-builder and the architect of the church as the director of the music and her right-hand man. It was not a dream at all. All that she had said the night before was in earnest. The architect and builder were present to see what alterations were necessary in the organ loft, to fit it for the new choir.

"I wish to have a large chorus choir, and that implies plenty of room. We were debating, Mr. Strove, as to what we should do with the organ. Have you any suggestions to make?"

The young man, with some hesitation, asked if it would be too much trouble to cut the organ in two, and to place it in the galleries on each side.

"A very good idea, sir. We will do it."

To Sebastian, the quiet manner in which the lady said this came as a new sensation. To spend hundreds, perhaps a thousand, dollars thus, in a moment, gave him an assurance of security and confidence. The lady really meant what she said. The splendid vision of the night before was a solid reality. He was really the director of the music, his very first wish had been accepted, and was to be acted upon.

The architect objected that, as the entrances to the galleries were in the front wall of the church, it would be impossible to put the organ there, as it would close the doors to the galleries. The organ-builder replied at once that the organ could be lifted up, and the entrance to the gallery could be made under the organ on each side.

So it was settled the organ was to be cut in two, and placed in the corner of the gallery on either side. The architect quickly drew a rough elevation of the organ in its new position, showing the passage-ways under the organ to the doors that opened upon the stairways in the towers of the church.

"Where will you have the organ-desk, sir?" said the builder.

Sebastian looked to Miss Brown, as if for instructions.

"Decide for yourself, Mr. Strove. You can have it anywhere you wish."

The young man thought a moment. If there was to be a conductor,—and it would hardly be possible to carry on a chorus without one,—he would face the choir, and the organist should be near him. So he decided the desk should be placed in the centre between the organs; and, if not involving too great expense, it would be better to have the organist sit quite near the front of the gallery, and facing the church.

"Expense is not to be considered," said Miss Brown. "That's decidedly the best place for the desk, and it will be placed there."

Then she turned to the architect, and had a somewhat lengthy conversation with him. The organ-builder considered himself dismissed, and went upstairs to his men, who were already taking out the front pipes of the instrument. Sebastian sat down in a neighboring pew to wait instructions from his new employer.

Evidently, expense was not to be considered. The music was to be of the best. There was to be a grand chorus, and, of course, a quartet of solo voices. What fine effects could be obtained by the union of the two! Of course, the choir would be large enough to admit of choruses by the male voices alone, or all the female voices. When he was a boy, on his father's farm, he had dreams of what he would do, if he ever became a conductor. Now he was something better,—manager of a fine church choir. His pulse quickened at the thought. Perhaps they would have some of the rich and highly colored music such as he had heard in Catholic churches. No: the people might not like that. And yet, why not? As the old master said: "If you praise the Lord, why not do it with joy and gladness, and with all the pomp and splendor possible?"

Presently, the architect bowed himself out; and Miss Brown came over to where he sat, and took a seat in the pew behind him.

"As I told you, sir, last night, I wish you to take control of the music of this church, under my direction. You will not find it a pleasant place at first. It was only with the greatest difficulty I got the congregation to consent to give me sole charge of the music. I think you will find that the present choir will oppose everything we do. It's of no consequence. I wish you to sing in the choir till the new arrangement begins in May. If you like any of the people in the choir, you may engage them for my choir,—in the chorus only. They are none of them good enough for soloists. Neither will the organist do for the new instrument. He may, however, do very well as the pianist.

"Piano! madam! Shall you have a piano in church?"

"Certainly. I shall have a grand piano and a harp, and occasionally an orchestra. I'll explain all these things in due time. The first thing I wish you to do is to organize a choir of men and boys, of not less than twenty voices. Then I wish you to collect a second choir of mixed voices, together with a third choir composed wholly of young girls. We will also have a double quartet of the best solo talent to be found."

"But, madam, think of the expense. It will cost thousands of dollars to maintain such an establishment. It will be as expensive as a grand opera company."

"I think I told you, sir, expense is not to be considered. It is your duty to provide what I wish. I'll attend to all the rest."

"I beg pardon, madam. The plan is so magnificent that it at first frightened me."

"Well, well, say no more about it. The organ-builder and architect think the improvements can be made in about two months. The organ is to be enlarged to twice its present size, and is to be fitted to a peculiar duty. You can call to-morrow at the factory, and see what you think of my plans."

She here began to draw on her shawl, as if to go.

"You will not fail to be at my house at three this afternoon, to sign the contract. Meanwhile, I shall insert an advertisement for singers, both boys and girls, men and women. I have arranged my music-room so that the rehearsals may be at my house; and you may say in the advertisement the applicants may call at my house to-morrow night, and you can try their voices in the music-room. Oh, by the way, the most important thing of all is to secure a soprano. Do you know of one?"

"Yes, I think I do; but, unfortunately, I do not know where she lives."

"Oh, you must find her. Ask at the music-stores. If she is the right person, I will pay her well. Good-morning. Remember. My house at three."

With that, she was gone. Upstairs, the men were busy taking the organ to pieces. Already the dust began to fill the church, and the sexton came in to open more windows. He seemed to recognize Sebastian, for he said,—

"Old Miss Brown have her way at last. She will make or break the church,— that's my opinion."

"I think she will make it: at any rate, I mean to help her."

"Lor! you're the new director she was talking about. I'm the sexton,— I am. I heard tell you would want new voices. I know lots of 'em, first-rate singers; and, if ye want to make a trade, I can help ye. Will charge 'em commission for the places, and divy on it."

The young man looked the old fellow full in the face, and then deliberately marched out of the church without a word.

The freedom of American life has had a marked effect upon music in this country. The liberty to do very much as he pleases has led the lover of music to do many things that are far from pleasing. In no other country do the people generally sing praises by proxy, delegating the songs of an entire congregation to four singers who sit apart in artistic reserve, while the congregation sit below in grim and critical silence, either pleasantly entertained by the show or idly wondering how much the music costs per note. Any other people would have first asked what was the best thing to do, and, having decided this, would not have stopped to consider anything else.

The American quartet choir is a compromise. The people do not choose to sing. They have a dim idea that four singers can give good music, and that they do not cost much; and so they pitched upon a choir of two men and two women as the correct thing for church music. In a certain way, they are right; for the four natural voices are united, and that is something. It is, however, much as if a painter had said: " Black upon white gives good strong, clear effects. I'll use no other colors." The result, as far as it goes, is good; but a picture in black and white alone is wanting in the charm of color. It is like a photograph, tiresome and unsatisfactory. The music of a church quartet is like a drawing in black and white. It lacks musical color, and is thin, tiresome, and uninteresting; and yet our churches are content with this cheap and poverty-stricken arrangement.

This was, in substance, what Miss Tabatha Brown said to Sebastian the day after their interview in the church.

"I have put an advertisement in all the daily papers, saying that you wished singers for your new choir. You are to represent me in this matter, and so your name appears on the advertisement."

With that, she handed him a newspaper. It was certainly an attractive advertisement: "*Wanted at once choir singers of both sexes, from nine years of age and upwards. Must be able to read at sight. Salaries payable weekly.* Apply at No. 97 West Sixty-third Street, Sebastian Strove."

"Number ninety-seven is the rear entrance to my house, and leads directly to the music-room. You will meet the people there, and try each voice for its quality and power, and examine each one as to their ability to read music at sight. This last test is essential, as I wish the music to be continually changed; and much of the music must, of necessity, be in manuscript."

The effect of the advertisement was remarkable. Two hundred and ten people of every age and condition applied at the door of the music-room before twelve o'clock, and before night there were one hundred and fifty more, and during the evening still another hundred. It was impossible to examine them all, and each was given a slip of paper on which was written the day and hour they might return for examination. The following day fifty more applicants appeared, and seventy applications by mail were received; and the next day after brought twenty applicants and more than three hundred letters. Every name was entered in a book, and every letter answered by postal-card, appointing a day for examination; and then the examinations began. Boys were received at nine in the morning, girls at two in the afternoon, and adults in the evening. It took four days to hear them all; and then the names of the successful candidates were announced in the daily papers, as a simple means of informing the entire nine hundred of their success or failure.

The standard established by Sebastian was very simple. The candidate must sing a piece of manuscript music of moderate difficulty, alone, without accompaniment, and at sight. He must also sing a printed second part to another voice, without accompaniment and at sight. The object sought in the new choir was to give new music every week, precisely as the players in an orchestra may give new selections every night. The quality and power of the voice being reasonably good, the whole question turned on ability to read. Of what avail is it if the voice is fluent, if it cannot easily, promptly, and correctly translate the thoughts of the composer? It is on this point that so much of our American musical culture is deficient. Any one who pretends to an English education is supposed to be able to read a newspaper aloud at sight. Why not the same in music? It is very certain if the singer or player cannot read ordinary music with equal ease, he is not a musician, however nimble his fingers or well trained his voice.

At the end of the week, Sebastian had only been able to select, out of nine hundred applicants, twelve boys, fourteen young girls, nine men, and twelve women. Scores of fine voices were passed with hardly any trial at all. Many came bringing songs which they wished to sing.

"I only want you to do one thing, read at

sight. If you cannot do that, I have no need of your services."

The extraordinary ignorance of this great mass of supposed singers was so discouraging that it seemed as if Miss Brown's scheme would fail, from a simple lack of the musical talent to carry out her plans.

"Never mind," said she: "we will advertise again in the neighboring towns. It will be extraordinary if we cannot find a hundred competent readers in the country."

On the Sunday, Sebastian resumed his place in the choir. The revolution in the musical affairs of the church seemed to be regarded by the other members of the choir as a personal injury. They would have nothing to do with the new scheme, and not one applied for admission to the new choir. They even darkly hinted of dreadful things that would soon happen. The organ was dismantled and could not be used, and this set the congregation to much thinking during the service and voluble remarks in the corridors after they had been dismissed. Not one had a good word to say for the unselfish woman who had set out to do what she could for the music of this church, and, as it afterwards proved, for the whole country. Sebastian did his duty, and made neither remonstrance nor reply. His day was at hand. It was better to do than to talk.

Miss Brown would not listen so quietly, and said with some spirit,—

"I have your written consent to this plan. I pay all the bills, and I propose to do very much as I please. Our church music is poor and thin. We do not use half the range of musical color. We are content with threads and lines, while we might have masses of color and broad and vigorous effects. Our church choirs need reforming; and, as the churches are unwilling or unable to do this, I mean to reform my own choir."

The minister, good and timid man, thought the scheme might be excellent, but it was entirely impractical. It might tend to detract from the sermon. As for the young person she had chosen to carry out her plans, he was not on visiting terms with any family in the congregation, and must be a person of no consequence whatever. Even the sexton, who had been so ready to turn a dishonest penny out of the affair, shook his head, and said the church was going to the bad. There were seventy pews to let in the church now, and, if the new-fangled music came in, there would not be ten people in the house.

For Sebastian, it seemed as if he had entered upon a new and beautiful life. His ideas, at first timidly offered, were respectfully considered and then acted upon. The first payment of his salary came promptly; and, thus relieved from anxiety, he began to make discoveries of himself. His mind worked quicker. New ideas, new plans and hopes and aspirations, came to him. He began to see the power of capital applied to art. If the lady would carry out his ideas, he would soon realize the dreams of his boyhood, and perhaps do something to render divine service more dignified and more beautiful by all the resources of music.

Miss Brown entered into all his plans with ardor. She was ready with new suggestions, and to his enthusiasm added experience and wisdom. He suggested that new music should be written for the choir, that a prize be offered for an anthem for the three choirs, so as to use them all in the manner of an orchestra; and she at once offered over $1,000 in prizes for new compositions suitable for church service.

The rumor spread through the country that there was to be a new and magnificent choir, and the singers in nearly every church in the city applied for places. The new advertisement brought out over four hundred candidates, and at the end of the second week the choir was complete except in soloists.

It was arranged in this way. First, there was a choir consisting of ten sopranos, six altos, eight tenors, and twelve basses. Secondly, there was a choir composed of sixteen boys, sopranos and altos, and twenty tenors and basses. Lastly, there was a choir composed of young girls only, six altos, six mezzo-sopranos, and twenty sopranos.

Every one was obliged to sign a contract to sing in the choir for one year at a fixed salary, payable every Saturday. They were obliged by this contract to sing twice every Sunday for fifty-two weeks, at Christmas and Easter and ten other special occasions, subject to the call of the director. They were also obliged to attend two rehearsals every week, and to submit to a fine for absence from church or rehearsal or tardiness in attendance at the hours named by the director. The contract was very stringent; and a few refused to sign it, and were dropped. As Miss Brown expressed it, "I propose to manage this affair to suit myself; I pay every one, and shall demand their services in any manner I wish. I am to be mistress, and not the choir. Mr. Strove represents me, and he is the sole authority in everything regarding the music."

It was a clever business arrangement, and, when fully understood, was readily accepted, and was faithfully carried out to the letter on both sides. Beside the choir, there was also a reserve choir that might be called upon at any time, so that the working choir was always up to its full complement of voices. These reserved singers were, however, to be paid only when employed. All the salaries and rehearsals began at once, though it might be many weeks before the first public appearance of the choir in the church.

Never had any young musician such opportunities. Never had director of church music such magnificent resources. Here was a fine large chorus of mixed voices, a choir of boys and men, and a strong female choir rich in fresh young sopranos. Either choir alone could give splendid musical effects. United, they would make a grand vocal orchestra. Contrasted, placed one against the other, boy sopranos against girl altos, boy altos with mixed female voices, or backed up by all the basses, the combinations would be endless, the effects full of perpetual variety and vocal color. He could put all the boys with all the girls' voices, put all the boys in the soprano part with the mixed chorus, or unite all the basses with the girls' sopranos, or all the male and female altos with the tenors or basses or both, or he could unite every voice in one splendid choir, rich in varied qualities of sopranos and with a strong bass under all.

The system of rehearsals for the new choir was arranged in this way. The male choir met on Monday and Thursday evenings. The mixed choir met on Tuesdays and Fridays, and the girl choir on Wednesdays and Saturdays. This arrangement continued for three weeks; and then they all met on Wednesdays and Saturdays, in this manner,— the female choir at six o'clock, the men and boys at seven, and all at eight o'clock. Each rehearsed for one hour, and then there was a rest for half an hour, and then all rehearsed together from half-past nine till half-past ten.

At the first rehearsals, each one received a book of practice music only, consisting of a selection of the usual styles of music used in churches, — chants, anthems, hymns, etc. Beside this, each received a number of sheets of manuscript music, each containing one part only. The idea was to treat the choir as an orchestra; and each singer had only his own part, and knew nothing of what others might have to do.

The first general rehearsal, when all were united for the first time, was a revelation in vocal music, a discovery in art, the opening of a new and splendid field in church music, something so novel and striking that the choir was instantly kindled to the highest enthusiasm for its new work and its new director.

The splendid music-room was brilliantly lighted. The girls' choir had met at six o'clock, the male choir came at seven, and at eight the mixed choir appeared, and for the first time they all met, and made each other's acquaintance. Sebastian briefly introduced them to each other, and then the mixed choir rehearsed alone. At half-past nine, the doors were thrown open, and Miss Brown, together with a brilliant company of invited guests, including the critics of the leading papers, came in and took seats. The chorus was arranged in a semicircle at the end of the room, the mixed choir in the centre, the male choir on the right, and the girls' choir on the left. A competent accompanist had been employed, and was seated at the piano in the centre of the half-circle; and Sebastian took his place upon a platform behind the piano near the centre.

When everything was ready, Sebastian called his forces to order, and thus addressed them:—

"Ladies and gentlemen, boys and girls, we have met for the first time as a new musical organization to try a new experiment in church music. You have in part made each other's acquaintance as three separate choirs, and I already feel you are inspired with a sincere desire to do your best to carry out the noble aims of the lady who has so generously established the organization." (There was a round of applause at this.) "There will be eight solo voices added in time, yet all are equal in the work, each one has an honorable share in the music; and, if we all generously work together, I think you will see that each and all may take pride in the new choir." (Again there was applause both from the choir and the audience.) "The first piece we will try is a simple psalm arranged for all the voices. You will read it from the manuscripts you have been studying for the past three weeks. Are you ready?"

CHAPTER VI.

O sing unto the Lord a new song! — Psalms.

OBSERVE the structure of the choir. It is essentially three choirs united, and is practically one choir with eleven parts. First is the adult mixed choir, in four parts; next, the men and boys' choir, in four parts; and, lastly, the girls' choir, in three parts, or apparently only nine parts, as the bass and tenors in the two first choirs are the same. In reality, they were not; for the bass of the mixed choir was considered a first bass, and the bass of the second choir was a second bass, making on the score laid upon the conductor's desk eleven real parts. It may be objected that this division of parts was only imaginary, and that the three soprano parts were really only one. The distinction is correct. The boy sopranos are a distinct part or voice, likewise the girls or women, precisely as in the orchestra the first violins and the flutes may and do play the same notes, yet no one thinks of calling them only one part in the score. This assemblage of singers, met under the direction of Sebastian Strove, and in the pay of Miss Brown, is believed to be entirely novel. It is divided according to the natural and well-defined qualities of the human voice, as found in men, women, boys, and girls. Every composer has written for these voices, and this is merely a union of them all in one vocal organization. This explanation is essential to a right understanding of the remarkable performance that immediately followed the speech Sebastian made to the singers.

It was a setting of Psalm xcviii. of the Common Prayer-Book, in eleven parts, as arranged by Sebastian from an anthem (in four parts) he obtained from a church music-book. The music itself was good, but of no special merit. Of this, we now care nothing, as the interest centres wholly on the vocal orchestration of the work.

It began with these words: "*O sing unto the Lord a new song; for he hath done marvellous things. With his own right hand, and with his holy arm, hath he gotten himself the victory,*" and was sung in the following manner: the sopranos of the mixed choir, which may be distinguished as simply the soprano, took up the first words as a solo, and were joined by the bass and tenor in trio on the second line. At the words "*hath he gotten,*" etc., the girl sopranos joined the melody. It was as if that part had been suddenly touched with a white light. The silvery brightness of the girls' voices seemed a second tone laid over the soprano, and yet part of it, and giving it an entirely new character. Those who were not occupied were struck with the effect; and there was a kindling of eyes and a sense of excitement that, had not Sebastian held them firmly in hand, would have been disastrous.

Small time for thought, for, with a sweep of

the bâton, all the tenors and basses were joined in four parts in a male quartet. The current of the music had widened and spread along the back of the choir. "*The Lord declared his salvation; his righteousness hath he openly showed in the sight of the heathen.*" The girls and women were startled by the abrupt change in the music; and some were so absorbed in listening to the music, they nearly lost their places. At the next line, "*He hath remembered*," etc., a portion of the tenors ceased; and the melody sprang to the boy sopranos, thus making a quartet of soprano, first tenor, first and second bass. Here was a new combination, a new quality of tone.

At the words beginning, "*Show yourselves joyful unto the Lord*," etc., the sopranos and altos were in duet. The next line, "*Praise the Lord upon the harp, sing to the harp with thanksgiving*," was given to the girls alone, in three parts,— soprano, mezzo, and alto. The effect of this sudden change, from boys and men to the close-wrought harmony and penetrating tone of the female voices, was not only wonderfully effective, but surprisingly beautiful. It was really an orchestral effect.

The next line, "*With trumpets and shawms,*" was by all the tenors and basses; and at the next line the melody was caught up by the girls' voices, the sopranos and mezzos being united. Here, again, was a new combination, a new tone color. At the line beginning, "*Let the sea make a noise,*" the mixed choir had the music in four parts. At the words, "*Let the floods clap their hands,*" the male choir joined them, the boy sopranos carrying the melody, and the boy altos joining the adult altos, with all the men in two parts only. At the last line, "*With righteousness shall he judge the world,*" etc., the entire choir was massed together, all the girls' voices being combined in the melody, and the boy sopranos taking to the tenor part.

For a moment there was a pause. Neither singers nor audience seemed to know what to do or say. The performance had been so unique, so unlike any choir music heard before, they were lost for words to express their admiration. Then there sprung up spontaneously a hearty round of applause from all present, except Sebastian. Miss Brown rose from her seat, and, coming forward, took him by the hand, and said, so that all might hear: —

"You have carried out my ideas to perfection, and in a manner that far exceeded my expectations. I must give you the credit of doing more with my plans than I thought possible."

This was followed by a hearty round of applause from the choir.

If the young man had been a city youth, he would have been greatly flattered, and perhaps upset and spoiled by such praise. He had been a student only, a dreamer and a recluse. He knew the toils he had passed through, the privations he had endured to get his education, and he knew his own shortcomings too well to be disturbed.

He said to his patron: "I thank you for your

good opinion; but it is, I fear, misplaced, or at least premature. The choir have not yet got to work, and they are not yet accustomed to this style of music."

"Then I am the more pleased," said the lady, with a smile. "If this is only the beginning, I do not know what new delights and surprises you will bring us."

Then she returned to her seat among her friends. As for them, they remarked among themselves that "this time Miss Brown had secured the right sort of lion, and that her ideas of church music would really come to something."

Sebastian turned to the choir, and said briefly: "I am much obliged to you for your approval, but let us not forget that this is the first attempt. Try to get accustomed to hearing the music move from part to part, and do not watch the others, but look out for your own work. You did very well for the first time, but we must not be content. We have much to learn before we are welded into a complete vocal orchestra."

The next piece was a hymn set to the familiar hymn-tune entitled *Germany*. There were four verses; and they were given without pause or interlude, by simply repeating the tune as a whole, but with a different arrangement of the voices each time. There was a prelude of only a few bars on the piano, merely to give the key and time, and not in any way suggesting the melody to follow. The hymn began with the melody of the tune by all the soprano girls. They sang one line only, and then they were joined by the girls' voices on the mezzo part, thus making a duet. The third line was a trio by the boy sopranos and altos and the second tenors. The fourth line was in full harmony, the boy and girl sopranos having the melody, the boys and mezzo girls having the alto, the girl altos and second tenors having the third part, and the second bass having the bass of the tune. The piano had the simple score of the tune, and gave the full harmony. This finished the first verse.

The second verse followed at once, the sopranos having the melody alone on the first line, and continuing it till the end of the verse. At the second line, they were joined by the boy altos and the first bass in a trio. The third line was a trio in parts, and arranged in this way,—sopranos and girls in the soprano on the melody, boys on the alto and the second tenors. The last line was massed up in four parts, with the sopranos, the soprano and mezzo girls on the air, the boy and girl altos united, and the second tenors and basses.

The third verse was treated more as a single melody, the first tenors giving the first line of the melody, the altos taking it on the second line, and the altos and the girl sopranos and mezzos having the trio in the third line. The fourth line was in four parts again, with both altos and mezzos among the girls on the melody, the altos taking their own part, and assisted by the first tenors and first basses.

The last verse was wholly choral, and began in the mixed choir in four parts. They had two lines; and in the third line, where the trio comes in the tune, the altos, sopranos, and tenors were joined by the boy sopranos and altos, and the second tenors, thus doubling each part. In the last verse, the entire choir was massed as a whole, the soprano and mezzo girls and the boy sopranos all being concentrated on the melody, and the other parts being simply doubled throughout.

It was difficult to say which were the most pleased with this performance, the listeners or the choir. The effect was so novel, so highly colored, and so varied in tone at every line, that it was like seeing a beautiful picture. The melody was always there, now in one part, now in another, the harmony continually shifting in tone, color, and yet fully sustained by the accompaniment that rigidly followed the construction of the tune. The tune itself is melodious, and readily lent itself to this orchestral treatment, the trio in the third line naturally suggesting a varied treatment of the parts.

It may be worth while to briefly observe the actual effect of such an arrangement of a tune.

The tune began as a solo, followed by a duet, in the pure silvery voices of the girls, with these words: "*There seems a voice in every gale, a tongue in every opening flower.*" At once, the melody moved to the boys and men in a trio with the third line, "*Which tells, O Lord, the wondrous tale,*" and instantly the music is fully choral on the last line, "*Of thy indulgence, love, and power.*" The boy sopranos and girl sopranos carry the melody, clear, bright, and incisive, over the rich harmony of girls, boys, and men, united on the other parts.

The next verse assumes an entirely different character. The adult sopranos carry the melody of the verse through: —

> "*The birds that rise on soaring wing*
> *Appear to hymn their Maker's praise,*
> *And all the mingling sounds of spring*
> *To Thee a general anthem raise.*"

On the second line, it is a duet between the

sopranos, boys and men. On the third line, this trio is reinforced by adding the girl sopranos to the melody, and the last line is choral; all the girls, except the altos, uniting on the soprano, and the girl and boy altos being united on one part, the whole sustained by the second tenors and basses. There the effect was entirely different, growing richer and fuller, the tune being really performed after the first line by men, boys, and girls, assisted by the adult sopranos.

The third verse began with the tenors on the line, "*And shall my voice, Great God, alone.*" The altos take up the line, "*Be mute 'midst nature's loud acclaim?*" The third line follows in trio with female voices alone on the words, "*No, let my heart with answering tone,*" when the first basses are added to these female voices to make a quartet, the two girls' parts being doubled on the melody. Here again is an entirely different tonal coloring, and fitting the sentiment of the words perfectly.

The last verse is choral throughout, growing

richer as it proceeds, the melody standing out clear and sharp with the three soprano parts united.

> *"And nature's debt is small to mine:*
> *Thou bad'st her being bounded be;*
> *But, matchless proof of love divine,*
> *Thou gav'st immortal life to me."*

Just at the conclusion of this piece, a servant entered and spoke to Miss Brown. She seemed somewhat concerned for a moment, and then the servant spoke to Sebastian,—

"If you please, sir, there is a woman below wishes to see you. She says she cannot wait."

Bidding the choir rest for a moment, he followed the servant past the curtained doorway into the dimly lighted parlor, and past that into the dining-room, where the servants were busily preparing supper, and then on into the hall.

Upon the carved oaken chair by the door sat a woman in faded black, dusty, travel-stained, and apparently bowed with grief.

"You wished to see me, madam — Oh!" And,

disregarding the servant; he took the woman in his arms as she rose, and kissed her thin, pale face. There was a rustle of silk behind him, and he turned to see who came. It was Miss Brown, standing in severe and frigid silence before them.

"Who is this person, Mr. Strove?"

"My mother, madam."

CHAPTER VII.

He, watching over Israel, slumbers not nor sleeps.—*Elijah.*

MISS TABATHA BROWN was a person of tact and kindly heart. She saw that Mrs. Strove had come from a distance, and met her son for the first time after a long separation. She called a servant, and bade him prepare the library for Mrs. Strove, where she could wait till the rehearsal was finished; and, telling Sebastian he might remain with his mother for a few moments, she ordered the supper-room to be opened, to divert the attention of the choir and her guests from his temporary absence.

The moment he was alone with his mother, Sebastian told her briefly what was going on; and she, taking in the situation, said nothing of her journey and arrival, except to explain that she had arrived alone in the city, and, going to his lodgings, had left her things, and had followed him to the rehearsal. The real reason of her appearance in the city she withheld till a more convenient season.

The choir sang twice after the supper, and then went home, highly pleased with their new employer, their young director, and themselves. Sebastian returned home with his mother in Miss Brown's private carriage; and, when they were alone at his lodgings, she told him all that had befallen her within the last few days. A tornado, such as are common in the West, had struck the house in the night, and destroyed it in a moment. His father and two brothers and his youngest sister were instantly killed. She alone had escaped, unharmed. His other brothers and sisters were employed and living in other places, and had escaped. The storm had also ruined the crops and overturned the orchards. None of his brothers or sisters were doing more than support themselves. Therefore, she had buried her dead, sold the ruined farm for a pittance, and had come to the East, to him, as her only stay in life. The news, dreadful as it was, did not move him greatly. His father had not been a true father to him. His brothers and sisters he hardly knew, except as children. His ways had not been their ways, and they had of late years grown apart.

Now was he glad of his success. He would take better lodgings at once, and his mother should keep his home for him. He told her all,— his good and ill fortune, omitting nothing, save the episode of his acquaintance with Zegelda Romanief. At last, all had been told; and the landlady kindly offered Mrs. Strove shelter for the night, and gave her the room lately occupied by Zegelda and her mother.

In the morning, Sebastian at once prepared to remove with his mother to better quarters. He would take a flat, and she should keep house for him till — till he found Zegelda. They went out to breakfast, and then returned to Sebastian's room. When they were alone, his mother drew from her pocket a soiled and faded photograph, while in her eyes there began to kindle a strange light, as when one turns over whitened ashes to find a glow beneath. Showing the card to Sebastian, she said,—

"My son, who is this person?"

He took it and examined it carefully, and even went with it to the window, turning his back upon her. It was a photograph of Zegelda, dressed in some fancy costume. On the card was the name of some photographer in Chicago, with a date of more than three years before.

"Where did you get it, mother?" said the young man, without turning round.

"I found it in the room where I slept last night. Do you know the child? Has she been here lately?"

The picture had sent the blood to his face, and filled him with sudden emotion. He composed himself as quickly as possible, and said with assumed indifference,—

"It is a young girl, a singer, who lodged here a short time ago."

"Did you know her, my son?"

"Yes, I knew her quite well. I saw her often, when she was here."

"My son, you are concealing something from me. Tell me all you know of this person."

He could not suppress the truth, and told her of his meeting with Zegelda and what he had done for her, omitting nothing, save the fact that he loved her. How could he tell of that? It was all so new, and perhaps he might never see her again. What use to confess he loved a girl who had disappeared no one knew whither?

"What was her name?"

"Romanief."

"Romanief! Oh, I knew it, I knew it! It is the same face."

She spoke quickly and with rising excitement.

He understood very little that she said, and sat gazing at her in surprise. After a pause, he spoke.

"I do not understand it, mother. You say you know the face?"

"I know this face! Oh, I did, I did! A mother well knows her own. Listen, my son, and forgive me, if you can. Once I was the only daughter of a clergyman in Worcester, Massachusetts. I was indulged in every wish, and was allowed all the freedom accorded to young girls in that secure and safe country. None could believe there were wolves in Massachusetts. Yet one came,— a music-teacher from — from none knew where. He opened a school in the town, and I was his pupil. He was very handsome,— oh, very handsome; and half the girls in the place lost their hearts to him. Mine he stole completely. I was mad, infatuated, and I loved him. He persuaded me to marry him, and I did,— secretly and against my father's wishes. For a while we were prosperous and happy, and we travelled much about the country. Suddenly, he deserted me in Cleveland, Ohio. It was when my only child was about one year old. He abandoned me, and took the child with him."

She paused, overcome by the recital, and there was a painful silence in the room. The shadow of disaster and misery seemed to be gathering about the young man. He seemed chilled by its shade. After an effort, he said as quietly as he could,—

"And you never saw him again, nor the child?"

"No, not once. I sold all the little property he had left with me, and travelled on in search of him and the little one. I lived in various towns through the West, and taught music for a living. I searched all the papers for trace of him, and I found nothing except an advertisement of a music school. I went to that town, but too late. He had gone; and there was a rumor that he had again played false with some poor girl's heart, and had been hunted from the place by her brothers, and it was thought he had been killed. The rumor grew to what seemed a certainty. He met his deserts; and after that — more than two years after that — I married your father."

"Why did he take the child?"

"I do not know, unless he thought he might in some way make her of use in his concerts. She had already, as an infant, shown a most precocious talent for music. For my part, I hate music. It is a snare and a bitter grief for all who follow it. I used to think it divine. I know better now. Men who follow music can be vain, false, selfish. It seems to destroy their manliness, and they become infirm of purpose and blind to truth and right."

"Hush, mother! I cannot hear you say that."

"It is the truth, my son. I have seen much of these concert-giving people. They are false and insincere. But I am forgetting. My dead past was not buried all these years. This girl, this singer in this shameful dress, is my child. I feel sure of it. She has her father's face. I must see her at once."

"I fear you cannot see her, mother. She is lost."

Then he told her of Zegelda's disappearance,

omitting nothing, and even telling of her fear and dread of the agent, Sill.

The story seemed to completely unnerve the woman. She was faint and ill, and was forced to lie down upon the bed. He soothed her as best he could with promises to find the girl, to bring her back again. He would go at once in search of — of this person.

Meanwhile, his duty called. The rehearsals of the choir took place every night. It was essential that the singers should become accustomed to each other and the new style of music they were to use. As the choir was wholly unique in composition, there was no music in print adapted to it, and nearly all the music had to be prepared for the choir in manuscript. This involved a great deal of clerical labor, which Sebastian at first undertook to do alone. Miss Brown observed that he was often preoccupied and restless, and, fearing he might be ill, offered to provide a music copyist and assistant.

"I see you are overworking, sir. That is dangerous in this climate. Take it more easily, and keep your mind at ease."

Hollow advice it seemed. How could he rest, how be at ease, and Zegelda, his love — no, his — He could not speak of it at all, but worked on in feverish anxiety, hoping, trusting, and yet fearing he might find her.

The time set for the first appearance of the choir was fast approaching. The work on the organ was nearly completed, and already in the church; and, in fact, throughout the city there was the greatest interest manifested in the new experiment in church music. The newspapers had given glowing accounts of the first rehearsal, and the plan of the choir was discussed in editorials more or less able. Some thought the scheme a good one, others were sure no good would ever come of it for the church or for art. The result was that Miss Tabatha Brown and her New Tenor, as he was called, were much talked about, which was really a matter of indifference to them both.

Sebastian still sang in the old choir; and, as it

was well known he was the director of the new organization, the members of the choir and the majority of the people treated him with a certain formal politeness, out of respect for his employer. At the same time, the opinion in the congregation was decidedly opposed to his plan; and many predicted the new choir would be a dismal failure, and that the church would be glad to return to its beloved quartet. The music committee were unanimous that the church would be deserted by all self-respecting Christians as soon as the brass band and opera chorus were introduced into the church. That was the way rumor had put it. The eccentric Miss Brown had completely lost her head, and intended to have a military band and a chime of bells with a monster chorus of one thousand voices. It was even darkly hinted that a drum-corps had been engaged. Even the minister, good man, deplored the proposed changes, and feared the service of song would be of a vain and worldly character, and ruinous to all interest in the sermon.

In all this, the young man kept up his search for Zegelda. Having secured a flat and made his mother comfortable, he took every hour free from his duties for this hopeless work. He felt sure she had not left the city. There was no better place to hide than in a great city. He appealed to the police; but they had no information concerning such a girl, and suggested he look for her among the music-halls and beer-gardens where young girls were sometimes employed to sing. He even hired a detective, but nothing came of it — save the expense. He wandered for miles through all the streets. He haunted the music-stores and piano-warerooms. None knew of her, none cared for her. A girl lost,— it was nothing new. Better let her go; that kind were not worth looking after. As for the agent, Sill, none of those who knew him had seen him for a long time. He had probably scraped together another deluded company of would-be singers, and had gone with them "on the road."

One night, after rehearsal, he wandered aimlessly down town, sick and weary with the hopeless search, and found himself, he knew not how, among a number of low beer-gardens where music is prostituted to lure the reluctant drinker. He passed several without thinking much about them, and then came to one more flashy and disreputable than the rest. There was a great crowd about the door; and, hearing a sound of applause, he went in to see what was going on. There was a long bar just inside the door, and at the upper end sat a fat and beery German, who seemed the chief bar-tender, talking with the agent, Sill. Beyond, over the heads of the crowd, could be seen the stage at the upper end of the music-hall.

Sill's back was turned to the door; and he did not see Sebastian, who came up to the bar and stood close behind him. He ordered something to drink, hoping to gain time to hear what the man might be saying.

"Tell you what, Somers, you can have the gal every night, from eight till one, with four songs for fifteen dollars a night, paid to me in cash."

"Fifteen dollar! Vat you say? Fifteen dollar!"

"Of course, man. Ain't she filling your place every night? You never had no such card before."

"Vat surity you gife me, Mr. Sill? Bimeby, the girl come not at all. How you make her come when she have a coldt? Dese young girls alvays has a coldt, ven dey sees dey is in demand."

"Never you mind that. I have a hold on the gal, and she will come every night,— sure thing."

"Den I makes it a drade, but, if the girl fail to come one time, you shall pay me one hundred dollar."

Just here the man turned and observed Sebastian.

"Hullo, Strove! What you doing here?"

"Oh! I merely wandered in out of curiosity."

"What you taking? Soda! Lemonade! Blue Moses! That's not the stuff for you. Come to a table, and I'll stand treat. I want to talk to you,— I do."

Thinking he might in some way learn something of Zegelda, he paid for the lemonade and left it untouched, and followed the agent through the crowd in the music-hall to a table. A waiter came at the call of Sill, took an order and a sly wink, and departed. Sill then began to be voluble over Sebastian's new choir and position, saying it was the talk of the town, and proposing a scheme whereby an honest penny might be turned out of the choir.

"Comish, my boy! Comish! That's what you should have out of that thing. You should make every singer pay comish for the place."

The servant here brought glasses and liquor that seemed to be wine and was something else. Sebastian could not refuse to drink with the fellow, as he hoped to gain some information from him, and he swallowed a little of the stuff. It was hot and bitter, and he drank as little as possible. Just then there was a noisy sound of applause, and he stood up to see what was going on.

"Oh, sit down! Sit down! Never mind that rubbish, it's nothing particular."

The wretched band began to play, and the laughter and noise died away. Suddenly there came a voice,—a woman's voice, sweet, pure, and wonderful, filling the place as with light. Sill had risen also, and stood before Sebastian as if to detain him; but he broke away, and dashed through the crowd toward the stage, overturning a waiter and his tray of beer on the way. In a moment, he was in the clear space before the stage. The air, thick and blue with tobacco smoke, seemed to stifle him, and he felt faint and dizzy. He guessed at once, and rightly, that the stuff he had drank had been drugged; and he brought all the power of his will upon himself to master its effects. Fortunately, he had lived a pure and temperate life, and was strong and well. At a bound, he was upon the stage by the singer's side.

"Zegelda! Zegelda!"

At once there was a howl of rage, and loud cries on every side: "Put him out! Pull him down!" A fat and beery brute sprung out from the side of the stage, and tried to push him off.

"Stand back!" he cried. "Stand back, or I will kill you! She is my sister."

In an instant, the music stopped, and there was an awful hush. The audience of half a thousand men and boys seemed to find themselves spectators of a tragedy.

"Kick him out! Kick him out!" cried Sill from the crowd.

"If you touch me, there will be murder," said the young man, turning a white and desperate face upon the crowd. "She is my sister! I lost her."

It seemed as if the vast throng had been suddenly changed from beasts to men, for there rose a roar of approval. Zegelda had paused in her song, and stood for a moment irresolute. Then she came to Sebastian, and said so that all might hear, —

"Take me home!"

This was followed by another roar of applause. It was as good as a play. They were bound to see it out, and with rough and ready humor bid the man on the stage retire. Then they made a lane down the middle of the room. Some one cried out,—

"Take the gal home, sonny. You're a good un!"

They stepped down from the stage, and passed up the lane between a swaying, tumultuous crowd of men, while the air was rent with shouts and screams of laughter and applause. They passed on toward the bar-room; but the people made way for them, though there were ill-suppressed murmurs on every side. At the door, with his back to the great window, stood Sill, with his hand behind him as if ready to draw a revolver. His face was black with rage and hate. It was clear he meant mischief. Sebastian glanced back toward the bar, and saw a man lift a heavy stone bottle to hurl it after him. He sprung aside, and the missile struck Sill full in the face, and he fell backward, with a fearful crash, through the window, and dropped into the street, covered with blood. At the instant, a policeman appeared upon the walk.

"Look lively, young fellow!" cried the officer to Sebastian. "Get out of this. There's going to be a bad row here."

CHAPTER VIII.

SEBASTIAN found a carriage as quickly as possible, and put Zegelda in it; for she was dressed in some fancy costume, with a silken cap upon her head. He bid the driver take them as quickly as possible to his home, and then entered the carriage with Zegelda. Hardly was he seated by her side, when the close air and the motion of the carriage, combined with the excitement he had gone through, and perhaps the lingering effects of the drugged liquor, caused him to faint. The girl was terribly frightened at this, and imagined he was hurt, and tried with all the skill she had to revive him, and at the same time covering him with passionate caresses, and appealing to him to revive for her sake. When the carriage stopped, she was obliged to call a policeman to assist her to take him to his rooms. At the door stood his mother, surprised, alarmed, and perplexed at the sight of this strange girl in such unseemly dress, bringing up, aided by the janitor and the officer, her son, pale and perhaps lifeless. She led the way in silence to Sebastian's room, and then she turned to the officer for explanations. He could tell her nothing, and went away. The driver was importunate for his pay; and, in paying him and in sending the too inquisitive janitor for a doctor, she forgot the girl. She closed the outer door, and returned to the chamber. There stood the girl, bending over Sebastian and bathing his forehead in water. Who was the creature? What had she to do with her son? What terrible and shameful disclosure was at hand? She saw a girl in most unwomanly dress, tending upon her boy; and she was filled with anger and dismay.

"Who are you, Miss? What do you wish with my son?"

"I am his friend," said she, without looking up. "Or, rather, he is mine. God bless him! He saved me at the risk of his life from worse than death."

"What right have you in his room? How came he to this? What right have you to call him your friend?"

"The best right. I love him."

With that, she turned and faced his mother, and pulled off the silken cap on her head. The woman stood as one frozen with amazement and alarm. She could not speak, but stood gazing at the girl with eyes in which tears vainly tried to well forth.

"Get me some ice water," said Zegelda. "I fear he has been drugged."

The woman did not move, but stood gazing at her earnestly; and the girl again turned to Sebastian, and bathed his face in silence.

"O my child! Do you not know me? I am your mother."

The girl looked at her for an instant in wonder, and then said slowly,—

"I don't know what you mean. I only know he saved me from that horrible garden, and I mean to stay here and help him. I will never leave him again as long as I live, unless he bids me. Now bring me the ice water."

"I am his mother, girl."

"Oh!"

Fortunately, the doctor arrived just then; and, in his presence, nothing more was said or done, except to minister to Sebastian's wants. The physician was evidently surprised to see Zegelda in such strange disguise, but he wisely said nothing. He calmed Mrs. Strove's fears concerning Sebastian, left a prescription for him, and went away, saying that the young man was not hurt and would revive presently. In fact, he did revive just after the doctor had gone, and sat up upon the bed, gazing in bewilderment upon the two women.

"What has happened, mother?"

"I do not know, my son. You were brought here senseless in a carriage by this young person."

"Oh, yes! I remember. If I had not dodged that bottle, I might have paid for my adventure with my life."

With that, he rose from the bed and walked into the next room. Zegelda followed him closely, and even came to his side and put her arms about him.

"How can I ever thank you? You saved me from that man. You will forgive me, will you not?"

"Forgive you! For what?"

"For leaving you, when you lost your place in the church. I was afraid I was a burden to you."

"Sebastian," said Mrs. Strove, with some severity, "who is this person?"

"Pardon me, both of you. Zegelda, this is my mother."

Then he stopped, and stood silent and irresolute before them. How could he say more,— how tell the child the claim his mother made on her, how explain to his mother his relation to this strange, strange creature, in such unwomanly dress? He thus stood, revolving these things quickly in his mind, when he felt a soft arm, warm and beautiful, steal in his. Her soft presence close to his side, her deep and burning eyes bent on his, filled every vein in his being with passionate love. She seemed to divine some impending disaster, for he saw her bosom rise in stormy agitation. Yet he must tell her of his mother's conjecture and claim.

"Zegelda, this is my mother. She was once your father's wife, and we think she is your mother also."

She started away from him, with blazing eyes. "It is false. My mother is dead!"

"Dead!"

"Yes. She died a week ago, in a miserable tenement down town. She starved to death. I might have followed her, had not MacCurry found us. He gave me food and this dress, and paid for my mother's funeral."

"MacCurry! Who is he?"

"The man you call Sill."

"My child," said Mrs. Strove, taking Zegelda's hand, "you have your father's face and name. I feel sure my child lives, and that you are — my little Mary."

"But my name is Zegelda. I was never called anything else."

"You were very young when I lost you. You may not remember. Yet my heart tells me you are my child."

"I do not believe it."

"Can you not prove your parentage, Zegelda?" said Sebastian. "Have you no papers, no documents of any kind."

"Documents! I don't know what you mean. O Sebastian, it can't be true. It cannot be true."

She came nearer to him, and seemed to cling to him for help and protection.

"My child," said Mrs. Strove, "I feel sure I am right. Sebastian is your brother."

"He, my brother, my brother! Oh, no, no, madam! That cannot be, for I love him."

"Zegelda! You love me?"

"Love you! How could I help it?" she cried in innocent and girlish frankness. "You were the first who ever spoke a kind word to me. You saved me from that man. Of course, I love you."

"Sebastian," said Mrs. Strove, gravely, "your sister excites herself unnecessarily. Bid her calm herself, and behave with more propriety."

* * * * * * * *

The next morning, Sebastian lodged a complaint with the Society for the Prevention of Cruelty to Children against Sill, and before night he was under arrest. An examination soon after, before a police magistrate, disclosed the fact that he had a contract, signed by Zegelda's father two years before, and giving her services to Sill as a concert singer for a term of three years. Six months of this contract had been served by her at the time the concert company broke up that winter's night, in the little town up the river. He had found her just as her mother died, and by threats had forced her to carry out the contract, and sing for him in the beer-garden. Alone by her dead mother's bed, almost starving for food, without friends or help, she had consented to sing for the man, well knowing he had no rights over her, and yet unable to resist his demands. The fact that the contract placed the girl in practical slavery to him, the fact that he had never paid either her or her father a cent under the contract, made it void long ago; but what could she do? Her position was not without example. Such things have been done before, and all the public sees is the face of a child musician smiling in a tragedy upon the concert stage. Nothing could be done with the wretch, except to take away the contract and wring from him a confession of what he knew of Zegelda's life previous to the breaking up of that wandering concert company.

CHAPTER IX.

Through darkness riseth light.— ELIJAH.

ALL things were now ready,— the choir thoroughly drilled, the alterations in the church completed, and the organ finished. It was the Saturday night before the first appearance of the choir, and Sebastian had gone down to the church early in the evening to see that all was ready for the final rehearsal. The janitor admitted him into the church, and he went upstairs to the organ-loft and lit one gas-jet over the desk. It was a curious scene. The church seemed like a vaulted cave, dim, strange, and vast. On either side of the great window that seemed to glow with subdued fire in the light of the moon, stood the painted pipes of the double organ. Beneath the window were the seats of the choir, rising tier on tier from the front of the gallery. The organ-desk stood in the centre near the front. Directly behind it was a grand piano, and beside it a harp covered with a hood of canvas.

The young man paused in thought before the scene. Here was the realization of all his dreams. His chance had come, his new life and work would now begin. The day was at hand, and through all the darkness of his life there was about to rise the light of love and joy. He had hoped Zegelda would come with him to the church before the rehearsal. He had much to tell her. She had gone out during the afternoon, and he had therefore come alone.

He opened the organ-desk, set the hydraulic engine in motion, and sat down before the keys. He would play, alone in the church, a solemn psalm for all the mercies that had blessed his life.

"Let us first see what we have here," he said

aloud, as he began to draw the stops. "An open diapason of sixteen foot tone (large scale), a second diapason, a doppel flute, a gamba, and trumpet, each of eight foot tone. Then a flute harmonic, an octave, and clarion, each of four foot tone. Twelfth, fifteenth, and three rank mixture. So much for the great organ, simple and yet strong, just the thing for such a choir. Now, for the swell organ," he continued, reading off the stops as he drew them out. "Open diapason, stopped diapason, viola, oboe, cornopean, flato traverso, violina, and a sixteen foot bordone. Enough for all the variety needed, and well suited to the wants of the accompanist. Pedal-stops, open diapason (very large scale), bordone, and trombone, each of sixteen foot tone, and a violoncello of eight foot. Last of all, on the swell manual, a tuba mirabilis, really a marvellous trumpet, fit to lead an entire congregation."

The organ is worthy of study. It was designed with care, to serve the purposes of this particular church and choir. It was a comparatively inexpensive instrument, costing only $5,600, $5,000 for the instrument and $600 for the reversed action brought to the front of the gallery. It will be seen that it is not a "show" organ, for the displaying of nimble fingers and the player's vanity or the tickling of congregational ears. It was a chorus organ, with just variety enough to furnish a background for the solo voices; very rich in diapasons and basses, and as a whole of dignified and church-like tone.

Having drawn every stop, the young man prepared to play alone in the church a psalm of praise for all the mercies that seemed about to crown his life. At the instant, he heard a moan. It seemed to come out of the darkness of the church. He stood up, and looked over the railing into the great, black cave below. There was nothing, save blackness and darkness. Again he heard it, plainer than before. It seemed to freeze his heart with vague horror and alarm. He cried out, and asked who was there. There was no answer, save a rustling sound, as if some one stirred in the darkness. He tore a leaf out of a music-book, twisted it into a taper, and, lighting it at the gas, went down the stairs and entered the church.

"Who is there?"

Not a sound in reply.

"Any one hurt? Any one here?"

His voice seemed lost in the darkness. There was not even an echo. The paper torch was fast burning away, and he went hastily up the main aisle toward the pulpit.

"Zegelda!"

The flickering light fell upon a girlish form, resting at full length, and apparently in helpless misery, upon the pulpit steps. He dropped the dying torch, and in the darkness, just touched by the distant lamp in the organ-loft, lifted her up and stood supporting her by the door of the first pew.

"How came you here? What is the matter?"

For a moment, she could not speak for sobbing. At last, she managed to say,—

"The janitor let me in — more than an hour ago. I heard you come in. I was afraid you would begin to play, — and — I could not bear it. O Sebastian! Is it true — is it all true as people say?"

"Is what true?"

"That — that God lives here. It seems so still, — so still and cold. I thought he must have forgotten me, and I came here — to remind him — of it all."

"Child, he never forgets. Come, sit down, and maybe I can tell you how he works for us."

She seemed to be soothed by his presence, and sat down beside him in the pew.

"Now listen, and see if I be right. This man, Sill, has confessed he stole all the money earned on that concert trip, when he abandoned your father and mother. He said your mother's trunk was left at the hotel at the little river town. I sent for it; paid the bill with interest, and this afternoon it came, and I broke it open. I wanted you to open it, but you were not at home, and I couldn't wait. In it, I found your mother's certificate of marriage to your father, and indorsed on the back with the date of your birth. Why, my child, you're only seventeen."

She said nothing for a moment, but he could hear her breath come and go quickly.

"Then I am not your sister at all?"

"No."

Suddenly, she slipped away from him out into the aisle; and clinging to the pulpit-railing, half-kneeling upon the stairs, she gave way to passionate tears.

"Oh, you will despise me! You will hate me."

"Why should I?" cried he, coming nearer to her.

"Can't you see? My father had no right— Oh! how can I say it — how can I say it?"

"Zegelda, I do not care. Shall the sins of the father be laid upon the innocent shoulders of the children. No. God will judge between us — with mercy."

"And you do not care at all — you will always — "

"I will love you all the same — now and always."

For a moment, they two stood in silence in that place. Then she said sadly, —

"Poor lost little one! It must have died. What will your mother say? She loves me already."

"And so she always will — as her daughter."

She moved away from him, and seemed to peer up into the dim arches faintly outlined overhead. One of the white angels with outstretched hands, in the dimness above them, seemed to glow with light, and its face seemed to look down upon them with a calm, sweet smile. Her vivid imagination made it all alive.

She pointed up at it, and said, —

"You are right. He lives here."

Then she turned and looked up at the organ.

"Come! There is my place. There is music, the only language that can tell all that is in my heart. Come, let us go up there."

They went hand in hand up the dim aisle and dark stairs, and came to the new choir-loft.

"How beautiful it all is! Sit down and play for me. My heart is full, and I must sing."

* * * * * * * *

The morning bells called the people to church. The moment the doors of St. Clement's were opened, a multitude poured into the place. In half an hour, every seat was filled; and still they came in throngs, blocking the corridors and filling the aisles in dense masses. When the minister came into the pulpit, he wondered greatly at the great congregation that had assembled. At first, he was disturbed. These were vain people, come with worldly curiosity to hear the new choir. Then he came to a wiser conclusion. He would have many listeners, and he must do his best.

In the new organ-loft, the choir had already assembled, and sat in solid rows clear back to the wall; the adult choir in the centre, the ladies in front, the male choir on the right, and the girl choir on the left, with the organist, the harpist, and pianist near the centre. In the front were the soloists, seven people, with one seat still vacant. There was an ill-suppressed buzz of excitement over all. Many were shocked at the sight of the piano-forte, others were positively indignant, all of which proves they were a trifle ignorant. A carriage drove up to the door, and Miss Tabatha Brown, anxious and troubled, stepped out. They made way for her in respectful silence, and she entered the church and spoke to the sexton.

"Yes, Miss. Mr. Strove has come. Here he is now."

"Oh! I'm very glad you have come. I am very anxious about the soprano. None of the people you have tried will do. I could hardly rest last night, thinking all might be lost for want of one voice."

"Have no fear, madam. I have found the soprano. Leave it all to me."

Already the organ began to peal through the church.

"I must, it seems. But, if she fails, I shall be greatly disappointed."

"Have no fear. She will not fail."

There was a slight stir in the choir, and every head was turned to see who came. It was the director. With him came a girl,— young, surpassingly beautiful, and with that divine light in her eyes that comes of love and happiness. This was his choir, she would be his soprano. She felt she had the voice, and that now, at last, it had found a worthy audience and a worthy theme. He led her to the vacant seat in front. The choir was complete.

Guided by some unseen signal, the choir rose and stood expectant, manuscripts in hand. The organ music seemed to shine and grow luminous and glistening. Few knew it was the added pianoforte.

The anthem was to begin. Miss Tabatha Brown's ideas were to be made alive, that all men see and understand. Suddenly, from the mazy measures broke forth a sweet and tender strain of girlish voices in close and intricate harmony, — *Oh, come, let us sing,— sing before the*

Lord! Then from all the men in four parts there rolled a slow and stately psalm,—*For his mercies are upon all that fear him.* It seemed to kindle the choir to life; and over the slowly measured psalm there ran, like liquid fire, a brilliant treble or obligato melody by the boy sopranos,—*Awake, my soul, and learn to sing his praise.* It then resolved into a quartet between the tenors and basses, the boy altos and girl sopranos repeating all the words in new music and in a new tone color.

Then the first basses took up a new strain,—*My soul had fainted for the Lord,*—and the adult altos answered back, *But he is ever nigh. His mercies are always near: they compass all his people like as the mountains stand round about Jerusalem.* This was a trio of most unique and pleasing character between the tenors, the boy altos, and all the girls combined on the melody.

Here was a true orchestration, a real and proper treatment of the resources of the human voice. The people were hushed and surprised beyond measure; and, when the voices stopped and the organ went on alone, there was a marked sensation of pleasure and satisfaction over all the house. The harp joined the organ in plaintive measures, and then the piano joined as if in a prelude. There was an almost painful silence over choir and people. A single stop on the organ seemed to take up a new melody. Was it the organ?

I cried to him out of the depth. He heard my complaint. Therefore will I praise his holy name forever.

Above the deep silence of the place rose a new voice,— a soprano unspoiled by "methods,"— rich, sweet, pure, and womanly. It seemed a soul with lips of fire. It caught up all hearts and chained every ear, because of its beauty and because it spoke the singer's heart. Then awoke the full-toned choir in answering strains. Once more the single voice alone, here and there touched and brightened by adding all the boy sopranos or all the girl sopranos upon a single word or line, a gilding of the solo by added voices in the same notes, yet was it so skilfully done that the solo voice was always heard, just as a beautiful form in plastic art may be decked with color without losing its charm of shape and outline. Still the anthem went on, till every voice joined in the full harmony; and yet that one soprano dominated all, was heard above all, singing its hymn of joy and gratitude.

Psalm and hymn and chant followed in due order, each a new source of wonder and surprise. The minister, having for the first time in his life a really great congregation, preached as he had never preached before. The reason was plain. He had the inspiration of a people pleased and satisfied with themselves, their church, and music.

To describe in detail the music given by this remarkable choir would fill a book. Enough has been shown to illustrate what it could do. The principle upon which it had been founded was proved to be correct. Its first performance stamped it a success. The very people who had opposed it and predicted failure were the loudest in its praise. The unselfish woman who had spent her money to try the experiment was the respected and admired of all. Her chief satisfaction seemed to be in playfully informing her friends that, "if she was crazy, it was a very delightful kind of craze." Her plans were proved practicable. Her director had made them a success. The church had now the advantage of the severe and solemn music sometimes used in the Episcopal service where boy choirs are used; it had all the richness and splendor of the Catholic music; it could use the stately chorals of the Lutheran Church, and still have the artistic effects of the quartet.

One in that great congregation, that morning, sat through it all, sad and yet serenely happy. She had lived to see her son's triumph; and, though her heart was heavy at the thought of the little one lost so long ago, yet it already leaned upon a new love and a new daughter.

The vocal orchestra maintained by Miss Tabatha Brown at St. Clement's was kept up for a year; and every contract was fulfilled, though it cost over twenty thousand dollars. At the end of the year, a change was made. The choir became a volunteer organization, and none were paid except four soloists, the director, and the three accompanists; and thus the expense was reduced to a comparatively small sum. So great was the demand for admission to the choir that it was easily kept full. To graduate from St. Clement's was a pass into any choir in the country. And so it was the choir entered upon a second mission in music, and became a great school of art.

www.ingramcontent.com/pod-product-compliance
Lightning Source LLC
Chambersburg PA
CBHW031453160426
43195CB00010BB/967